'What a wonderful book! Kudos to Margaret Rooke for helping bring the insights and wisdom of these remarkable young people to the world. *Dyslexia is My Superpower* is a great read for children and parents and teachers and classrooms.'

– *Fernette Eide, MD, co-author of* Dyslexic Advantage

'Reading *Dyslexia is my Superpower* was entertaining, enlightening, educational and brought me to tears more than once!

When I was at school I often assumed, wrongly, that I had a problem, that I was somehow different, stupid or weird. I am different – I am dyslexic – but it is that difference that makes me who I am and it is indeed an attribute. Like many others a dyslexic brain is capable of working at 100mph, the only difference is that a dyslexic brain has to learn how to navigate the roundabout that has been put in the way.

Reading about other dyslexic kids' experiences would have helped massively when I was at school, but of course it would also have helped if I'd been diagnosed before reaching the age of 35 and having already completed two degrees.

This amazing book will let dyslexic kids around the world know they are not odd, they are not stupid and they are most definitely not alone. But more than that I hope it teaches teachers how to help dyslexic kids to reach their amazing full potential.

As Morgan from Tennessee said, "I'm happy I have dyslexia." Me too Morgan, me too!'

– *Judy Puddifoot, MRCVS BVet Med, MSc, BSc,*

'Students with dyslexia may struggle in the education system each and every day. This book embraces dyslexia and knows that every child can unlock their potential to succeed!'

— *Deborah Hewes, editor of* Embrace a Different Kind of Mind: Personal Stories of Dyslexia *and DAS Head of Publicity and Publications*

'This book fills an important gap in the literature about dyslexia. Kids with dyslexia will see themselves reflected in the pages. I'm getting this book to share with my daughter.'

— *John Rodrigues, author of* High School Dropout to Harvard

'This book made me smile, repeatedly. It gives voice to dyslexic children, showing all the success traits we know their dyslexia has conferred. They are wise, funny, creative and ambitious. It is also a poignant read as some of the older children describe the limitations put upon their ambitions. Teachers enter the profession to develop their charges, not thwart them. These young voices show the huge difference knowledgeable and sensitive teachers make and the devastating effects of ignorance. They show the significance of the campaign to get dyslexia awareness into initial teacher training. I think this book should be on the reading list for all teacher training courses.'

— *Margaret Malpas, MBE, Joint Chair of the British Dyslexia Association*

DYSLEXIA IS MY SUPERPOWER

(MOST OF THE TIME)

by the same author

Creative, Successful, Dyslexic
23 High Achievers Share Their Stories
Margaret Rooke
Foreword by Mollie King
ISBN 978 1 84905 653 3 (hardback)
ISBN 978 1 78592 060 8 (paperback)
eISBN 978 1 78450 163 1

of related interest

The Illustrated Guide to Dyslexia and Its Amazing People
Kate Power and Kathy Iwanczak Forsyth
ISBN 978 1 78592 330 2
eISBN 978 1 78450 647 6

The Self-Help Guide for Teens with Dyslexia
Useful Stuff You May Not Learn at School
Alais Winton
ISBN 978 1 84905 649 6
eISBN 978 1 78450 144 0

I Don't Like Reading
Lisabeth Emlyn Clark
ISBN 978 1 78592 354 8
eISBN 978 1 78450 693 3

Self-Fulfillment with Dyslexia
A Blueprint for Success
Margaret D. Malpas
ISBN 978 1 78592 198 8
eISBN 978 1 78450 472 4

DYSLEXIA IS MY SUPERPOWER

(MOST OF THE TIME)

Interviews by

Margaret Rooke

Forewords by
Professor Catherine L. Drennan and Loyle Carner

Jessica Kingsley *Publishers*
London and Philadelphia

First published in 2018
by Jessica Kingsley Publishers
73 Collier Street
London N1 9BE, UK
and
400 Market Street, Suite 400
Philadelphia, PA 19106, USA

www.jkp.com

Library of Congress Cataloging in Publication Data
A CIP catalog record for this book is available from the Library of Congress

British Library Cataloguing in Publication Data
A CIP catalogue record for this book is available from the British Library

ISBN 978 1 78592 299 2
eISBN 978 1 78450 606 3

Printed and bound in Great Britain

MIX
Paper from
responsible sources
FSC
www.fsc.org   FSC® C013056

To everyone who is part of this book:
seize the day!

Contents

Foreword

CATHERINE L. DRENNAN

'May I ask you about your experience with dyslexia so that I can better advise my daughter?' one parent of a dyslexic child asks me. Another parent wants to know, 'Did you have a lot of trouble with school when you were young?' Also, 'Do dyslexic people view the world differently?' And, most importantly, 'How did you end up becoming a professor at one of the top universities in the world when your dyslexia was so severe that you needed to repeat a grade?' I try to answer each question to the best of my ability, but I remind these parents that I can't really say what the 'typical' experience is for a dyslexic child.

In *Dyslexia is my Superpower*, Margaret Rooke goes to the source to learn about the experiences of dyslexic children. In total, she interviews 100 children from more than seven different countries. The book is a collection of these interviews, in which children (aged 8 to 18) do their best to explain how they feel about being dyslexic.

'Dyslexia for me is like having a superpower,' says Morgan, age 10, an opinion held by many of the children interviewed. Elliot, age 17, credits dyslexia for an ability to 'tackle problems in ways other people can't'. Many others comment on increased 'creativity'. Personally, I have no doubt that my dyslexia has contributed to my professional success in the field of structural biology. Part of my scientific research requires aptitude in shape recognition, and through my years of struggling to learn how to read, I became an expert in shape recognition. Now I apply those abilities as a professor at MIT.

I think Molly, age 16, sums it up well: 'Sometimes I wish I could spell things more easily but most of the time I wouldn't change [being dyslexic] for the world.' This book is a must-read for parents of dyslexic children and for anyone else who wants to be uplifted. The 'superheroes' interviewed by Rooke are ready to take the world by storm. They are compassionate, hard-working and fascinating young people, who will most definitely make this world a better place. 'The best thing for me about dyslexia is that I have to try harder... Determination keeps me learning. I never give up. I always keep trying,' says Luke, age 10. Go get them Luke!

Catherine L. Drennan, Professor of Biology and Chemistry
at the Massachusetts Institute of Technology,
Massachusetts, USA

Foreword

LOYLE CARNER

In my early days at school I got quite used to being treated like I was stupid. Teachers would complain when I read in front of the class because I was slow and often made mistakes.

Because of my dyslexia I was always told how unlikely it'd be for me to find work as a writer. This frustrated me because I understood almost everything we studied. I knew how to articulate what I was learning verbally, but when it came to writing it down it would take me a lot longer than everyone else.

I found all of English tough: spelling, reading and grammar, but I loved writing. I think that's why I latched onto poetry and then later rap. With poetry and rap, the spelling and grammar doesn't matter. In my eyes it's written to be heard, not read.

One of my all-time favourite poets, a man called Benjamin Zephaniah, is dyslexic. I used to watch his videos

13

on YouTube religiously when I was younger; he became a
real hero of mine, defying the odds and carving out a career
in the one thing he'd been told he shouldn't pursue. He's
also written countless brilliant novels, all of which I've read
(admittedly very slowly).

I did also have a handful of amazing teachers during my
time at school. The first was a woman from the special needs
department at my first secondary school, Mrs Glenin. She
reinstilled in me a lot of the self-belief that had been worn
away by years of more impatient teachers.

The second was Mrs Baggott and, much like Mrs Glenin,
she simply trusted me and was always challenging me. She
kept my mind engaged and appreciated my work for more
than just the spelling mistakes. She understood that my
way of learning was different to some of my peers and she
catered for that in a very subtle way, without making me feel
like I was the odd one out.

The best teacher I've ever had, however, is my mother.
She works with kids with special educational needs. She
never taught me at school, but she was the one who taught
me exactly what my dyslexia was, how it worked and how I
could channel it and make the words that were in front of me
an ally instead of an enemy.

I think this is what helps all children with dyslexia and
other special educational needs – somebody to help them
fully understand how their superpower works, and how best
to channel it positively. And, of course, someone to believe
in them. One of the most important features of this book is
the information that children are giving teachers about how

to teach in a way that suits them and can help them learn. Nobody knows what works for a child with dyslexia better than a child with dyslexia.

I've never really felt any pressure to succeed, besides the pressure of having to make money. I've tried to build everything with my career slowly and organically. I was very lucky to have a mother who believed in me and trusted my judgement. If it wasn't for her I wouldn't have dropped out of university and given this music lark a go.

To anyone struggling with dyslexia – including the kids in this book, who explain their experiences so beautifully – the most important thing I can tell you is that you are not stupid. Your mind works in a different way, that is all. Never think for a second you are any less than anyone else in your class. So what if it takes you longer to read something, or your spelling isn't brilliant?

On top of that, though, what I really want to tell anyone struggling with dyslexia is I really struggled to write this. I struggled to put my frustration with dyslexia down in words. But if you were to ask me face to face I'd have no trouble explaining it to you. Just because I'm a slow writer doesn't mean I'm a slow thinker. I think I'm one of the only people from my English class who now gets paid to write, and I was treated as if I was the only one who didn't know how. Hopefully this book will show you you're not alone, but instead part of something very special.

Loyle Carner, rapper, Mercury Prize nominee 2017,
London, England

Acknowledgements

Thank you to the wonderful Jessica Kingsley for the idea for this book. It has been a pleasure to work with you and the team at JKP again.

Thanks to everyone all over the world who has shared their stories and contributed illustrations, and to your parents and teachers for their support. Thanks to the organisations that have helped me (full list at the back of the book) and to Mylene McGuire, Katie Carmichael, Kate McGeever, and all friends and family for your encouragement. Special editorial gratitude to wordsmith Sarah Neville. Special thanks to my agent Jane Judd for your strong background presence.

Thank you Mum and Dad for always being so interested in my writing, and thanks and love to Terry, Loretta and Shea.

Introduction

Many books have been written about dyslexia, but perhaps the biggest experts are the ones whose voices are heard the least. All over the world, adults are making decisions for children with dyslexia: parents, teachers, politicians, education policy-makers...yet the needs and experiences of the young people on the receiving end of all this activity are not always understood.

For this book, I interviewed more than 100 children from many different countries – the USA, Canada, India, Australia, New Zealand, Singapore, the Caribbean, the UK and Ireland – to hear what they think is going wrong, and what is going right. They told me about their worst times and their best, their anxieties, their passions, their ambitions and dreams.

Almost universally, they loved to be listened to. We can be so focused on passing our own wisdom and experiences on to children that we can forget how much we need to ask them. Those I spoke to had very clear thoughts about what has worked for them in education and what they would like to see improve. Their imaginations were boundless: I loved hearing about Lucy's cockroach obsession and how Addison views a car: not, as I do, as a vehicle that gets me from A to B but as a series of processes that brings its engine to life. There is true irony in Elliot's dismay that by bleaching paper from its natural buff colour to bright white we make it harder for many with dyslexia to use, hence the need to dye it back again to help them read.

The patterns that came through in their answers surprised me. I expected talk of sporting and artistic skills, but other strengths were clearly apparent. Many said that maths was both a mystery and a misery in their lives while others were clear that maths is what brightens their school day.

Many spoke of their love of animals and the solace they gained from them and hopes of working with them in their adult lives. Others similarly spoke of 'hands-on' hobbies and potential careers. Lego® is a clear favourite. Several speak about wanting to delve into archaeology because of its physicality. Corinne in particular mentions the fingerprints sometimes visible on some newly discovered fragment of pottery.

A movingly large number of the children want to be teachers, often expressing a strong desire to help others with dyslexia. In reading this book, it's important to remember how many who are not included here go through the education system unrecognised and undiagnosed. Several of the young people I have spoken to have put presentations together to educate the staff at their schools about what they and others like them need. They feel it is imperative to teach the teachers, and most teachers have responded wholeheartedly to this.

I believe that children know their strengths. We can spot these by looking and listening. It's easy to get distracted by exam result pressure and grim parents evenings (I speak from personal experience as the mother of a teenager with dyslexia), but underneath all of that is a child who knows what they love and needs us to hear this. As one mum said to me, 'I thought I was praising my daughter but then I realised I needed to be more specific. I needed her to know how much I recognised who she is as a person and what she excels in.' How vital that we don't neglect to see how important these talents are. They could, after all, lead to a child's future career as well as engendering a great deal of personal satisfaction.

This book shows that each child experiences dyslexia in their own way. There is much common ground and much that separates them. Parents who have dyslexia themselves will know that, in some ways, they think and behave differently from their children.

It's not always easy to listen well. Another mum told me, 'A parent strives to understand their child's issues in order to support them but there is a lot of emotional baggage and defensiveness blocking this communication. Our own fears and anxieties can get in the way.' She added, 'Many children do not want to confide in their parents and this can be truer still as they get older. It will be useful to read about other children's experiences in their own words as this may help me understand more clearly what my own child is experiencing.' This mum felt there was something of a stigma attached to dyslexia when her son was diagnosed eight years ago: 'It would have so helped me to read about other children's experiences, their successes and setbacks, and their coping mechanisms. It would have made me feel less isolated and it would have shown me that my son was far from alone. He is one of a creative, colourful army!'

Dyslexia is a collection of attributes. Because of the particular nature of academic testing, it can be viewed as an affliction, but this is the fault of the academic testing, not the children. If academic life were different, dyslexia might show up as an asset, which can certainly happen after school.

Ashley Tejeda, a dyslexia teacher at an inner-city school in Texas, USA, says:

'Absolutely the people who make the decisions should listen to kids! They should also listen to adults with dyslexia. It is hard to make decisions on something you have never experienced or do not understand. In this case, the kids are the experts. There is wisdom in a counsel of many. Gather as much information as you can before making a decision.'

Tejeda adds:

'Most people learn a certain way and so that is how teachers are trained. However, some people don't learn that way. They need a specific way of teaching given by a teacher who understands that learning style. Most of them are extremely bright and have become highly frustrated due to their inabilities in reading or other areas. You can't teach someone who does not feel safe or who is sad or angry. Education should help children seek out how their gifts can benefit the world around them. It should show them that they have something unique no one else can offer. How can education accomplish this? Let's ask the children what they think.'

Pennie Aston, of the dyslexia counselling service GroOops, agrees:

'Through listening to our children we are able to access the world as they perceive it, not as we have learnt to believe it is or indeed, how we would like to think we are making it. In our work with young people we are so often told by referrers that dyslexic youngsters needed to learn to concentrate, to gain social skills, to control their anger and so on. What we found were sharp-minded, creative, social and quirky individuals, who were on the brink of becoming disillusioned and mistrustful of those entrusted to support and advise them.

By listening to our children's needs we have the opportunity to challenge outdated perceptions; to refresh our educational system. We can revolutionise the negative experience of school experienced by so many, the cost to society when the emotional repercussions impact in later life and, potentially, devise interventions that accommodate the strengths of the ten per cent rather than exclude and denigrate them.'

This is not a 'bash the teachers' book. Individual teachers clearly have a highly positive impact, and some schools, too, have put in place excellent, dyslexia-friendly systems. Elliot, from Stirlingshire, adds, 'The Scottish government has a system for reaching out to young people in local authorities to help them change and affect different teaching methods. We are raising awareness of the support needed and the conditions that affect Scottish students and we can also affect government policy on how government provides support for inclusion.'

Any other politicians listening?

Some of this book is painful reading. It is tough to hear about bullying and children blaming themselves for failing to learn. Yet it's enlightening to hear how they build their strengths and their capacity to cope and thrive. I hope you will find the book encouraging and inspiring. Perhaps together we can begin to create a sense of solidarity with all those struggling and succeeding with dyslexia around the world.

1

Dyslexia is my superpower

'My brain is shot by a lightning bolt of smartness.'

Jed, 10, Texas, USA

I feel like my brain is created in the way no one else's is. I think of a brain being shot by a lightning bolt of smartness. It explodes with a boom and my mind is blown.

I have something that most of the other kids in my class don't have. It's how my mind works in a certain way. One example is when I'm asleep: I dream of making an invention. Once I invented a flying car. In another dream I created a little gun that drills into the wall and then grabs inside the wall. Then you are lifted up with rope and get to places you can't reach or climb to, like a really, really steep hill. If you are falling down a cliff you can use it to get back up again.

There are a lot of things I'm good at – swimming, science, math, and researching lots of facts about animals. I love animals. In my free time all I do is watch movies that help me research about animals. Maybe it's because there are so

Courtney, 15, London, England

'Our inspirations and our imaginations are boundless.'

many things we still don't know about them and there is so, so, so much to learn. It's amazing what animals can do: cheetahs can run at 70 mph; the lemon shark is the fastest shark in the ocean.

My mom says you can pick three things you might want to do when you leave high school. I want to be a person who trains sea animals to do tricks or a musician or a chef.

I have a special thing for cooking. My mom gives me food to eat and, if I don't know the recipe, I can give a good guess about the ingredients even if I can't see them. I can taste a hint of garlic or spices or lemon.

School for me now is in between easy and hard. When I first went to school it was really, really hard. Reading was hard and writing and spelling were hard. My teacher once told me that my spelling was very creative!

I remember feeling kind of disappointed in those days. I knew how hard it was for me and I could see how easy it was looking at it through anybody else's eyes. I felt like I was having the hardest time. Every day I had a stack *this high* of work to finish. This meant I couldn't go out at recess. I didn't have very much time to play with my friends. Nobody talked to me about all of this but they could see that school was hard for me so they knew to let me be.

I have always told my mom and dad how school has been whenever I have had a hard day. Sometimes when I talk to my parents about it I even cry, letting it all flush out. Things aren't as bad now as the olden days, but it still happens sometimes.

I have been going to a special dyslexia class that really helps me work on my reading and writing and helps me not have such a big stack on my desk. That stack has pretty much gone now.

Alexa, 8, Vale of Glamorgan, Wales

There are four other people in my class that are dyslexic. I am in a gang with the others. Sometimes we do fun little dyslexic games. Everyone knows we have dyslexia so there is a sort of connection there.

Morgan, 10, Tennessee, USA

I have epilepsy and a lesion in my brain and I am a positive person. I see people with disabilities as the same as everyone else. God makes everybody the way that he wants to make them, so we are all special.

I think that because I'm dyslexic I'm more creative. Because I am dyslexic I know I can write differently. I can draw, colour and create. I can figure out a problem from the beginning. It makes me feel more calm and excited about being dyslexic. I'm happy I have it.

Morgan, 10, Tennessee, USA
'Girl with a book.'

Dyslexia for me is like having a superpower. People can see me but they don't understand how I do what I do.

Maybe they are jealous, or sometimes they make fun of
me, but I know I have a real gift to see the world differently.
Thomas Edison didn't start school until age ten and after a
few weeks he started home-schooling. He was too smart
and creative for regular school. I hope I'm a bit like him. He
made the first movie camera. I see the world like a movie – I
see movies in my mind by thinking of an idea and playing it in
my head.

One thing I love to do is design animal habitats. We have
a lot of animals in our house: a hamster, two dogs, a cat
and a turtle. I make them homes out of cardboard. I recycle
everything and never want to throw anything away. I like to
design clothes for people. We've got a sewing machine and
we're going to get making things with that.

The people that help me with my dyslexia and my medical
conditions are my mamma, dad and sister. They help me with
stuff that I can't do easily, like reading. I have mirror dyslexia
and dysgraphia so my writing and reading are perfect but
reflected backwards.

In kindergarten I felt I was going backwards. I wished I
was like the others, finding things easier. I was a little bit sad
and I was angry about it, wanting to be the same.

Mamma teaches me at home now and she tells me to
call her by a different teacher's name each year. This year
she is Mrs Snickerbottom because she likes Snickers bars!
If I say, 'Mom, I can't do this', she says, 'Not Mom – Mrs
Snickerbottom', and that makes it fun and it encourages me
and I don't feel defeated. Overcoming my difficulties makes
me a stronger person.

Elliot, 17, Stirlingshire, Scotland

Dyslexia allows me to tackle problems in ways other people can't. It's one of my defining features. I wouldn't give it up for the world.

I have never had a moment when I haven't been happy I was dyslexic. I have been frustrated – I had ten attempts trying to spell 'minutes' recently and then I had to Google it – but if there was a cure

> Ideas shoot from my head and I come up with out-of-the-blue solutions to problems and difficulties.

I wouldn't take it. It defines who I am, the way I look at the world and the way I deal with things. I visualise the answer to problems. Ideas shoot from my head and I come up with out-of-the-blue solutions to problems and difficulties.

I was always the worst at Maths, the worst at English, the furthest back on the Chip and Kipper books, and the last to get on to the Magic Key series (the popular children's reading series) at primary school. I hated reading. My parents tried throwing books at me but nothing helped.

My primary school teacher started to realise I wasn't just slow and she got my mum involved. She held out some pieces of work and said to my mum, 'You wouldn't be able to read it unless you knew what it was meant to say.'

It wasn't that I was struggling with concepts; just with putting pen to paper. So when I couldn't write 'water' when I was eight or nine, I wrote H_2O instead.

At the time the speech and language therapist in the primary school I was from didn't believe in dyslexia.

Luckily we moved house and came here and I went to Dyslexia Scotland.

One of my strongest memories is the grin I had on my face when I found out I was definitely dyslexic. I wasn't just not very good at spelling; I had a reason for not being good at spelling. It was one of my best days.

Other kids had known I was struggling in primary school. It was quite obvious when it came to doing maths. We would stand in a line with the teacher facing the front of the queue. The teacher would ask, 'What's 9 x 12?' If you got it wrong you would go to the back of the queue and I was always there. I still can't remember my times tables. I can't quite place the information together.

I do sense the anxiety when I can't spell a word. What would take someone else five minutes to write would take me half an hour. My writing's really slow without spell check. My handwriting's pretty much illegible.

I will always be grateful to the learning support staff at school: amazing people who aren't paid enough. At my school at the moment the numbers have gone down and a lot of them are part-time. Without them I would never have been able to achieve what I have done academically.

At the moment I'm doing Advanced Higher Biology. You have to do an experiment that is a proportion of your grade. Instead of doing something boring I decided to do something ridiculously complicated – making oxygen to feed a locust. I show that by supplying constant oxygen the locust will grow larger than those who don't get this.

I want to work in plant genetics. I think a lot of the attitudes to genetically modified food are based on a lack of knowledge. We are facing big increases in population – 10 billion people by 2050. We are going to run out of food. So many environments are unable to be used for growing food because of the harm we are doing with pesticides and herbicides.

There are always things that your dyslexia will make more difficult but there's nothing you can't do – it takes a different approach and some more effort and persistence.

> **For everything made more difficult for you to do there will be something that you find easier than everyone else.**

Dyslexia is a great tool for allowing yourself to achieve things by different means. It gives you the opportunity to look at the world from a different perspective. I just wish I was born in the 18th century when no spellings had been defined.

For everything made more difficult for you to do there will be something that you find easier than everyone else. It's finding what your strengths are and applying these, and finding coping strategies that are best for you.

I'm always thinking about stuff. I can never turn my brain off. I am quite skinny and do no exercise. I think it's because my brain is using up all of those calories. It's the brain power.

Ryan, 12, County Kildare, Ireland
'Dyslexia is my superpower.'

Ryan, 12, County Kildare, Ireland

Dyslexia gives me superpowers. That's the way I look at it. It changes the way my mind works. Anyone who is down on themselves for being dyslexic I would say to them that even some celebrities have dyslexia: really successful people. Lots of other people have too, so don't feel left out.

I went to some dyslexia classes and the teacher told me people with dyslexia are very intelligent and very good at figuring how to work out problems. I think this is true. Say someone's giving out to me and being annoying to me, I would go to the person and try to figure something out. I'd find a way to deal with it.

I think dyslexic people are way more creative. I know that if I draw a picture I draw it in very good detail. I've also heard that people with dyslexia are very good at listening. If someone is trying to describe something, maybe the person with dyslexia is the only one who is paying attention to all the detail.

One of my superpowers is that I am good at knowing how people feel. Everyone always says that I am very friendly and kind and good at caring for people. That might be something I have learned from having to think differently because of my dyslexia.

I found out I was dyslexic when I was eight. I was finding maths hard at the time and was finding reading and spelling hard too. I went for some tests. I was told to spell out and write some words, and figure out sums.

At school my teacher knows I'm dyslexic and he helps me and another boy who's dyslexic in my class, probably more than any of the others. He checks that we understand the work, but he doesn't do this in an embarrassing way. I also get extra help at school, half an hour every day.

Now I'm good at reading and spelling though I still find maths difficult. Reading bedtime stories with my mum has helped too.

I'd say to parents don't think your kid is really different and he needs lots of help. They will need some help but don't make too big a deal of it. Remember that everyone is different.

2

Learning compassion

'I want to help other people who are struggling.'

Leah, 14, London, England

I think, no matter how many struggles people go through, without them they wouldn't be the people they are. I know how it feels to get hurt or be embarrassed about something. As a result of this, I'm very caring. I think there needs to be people like me who care for others. Some people, when their friends are upset, they don't give a toss. I like to make sure people are okay.

When I leave school, I want to work with youth centres or in counselling. I want to make sure people get help and know where to go to find it.

Before this year I felt differently about dyslexia, but now I don't see it as a bad thing. I know now that people have to accept me for who I am.

In primary school my English was really bad. In reading I jumbled up my words a lot. I remember once when I was eight or nine the teacher saying we had to write down our work on the computer. I kept on trying but I couldn't focus because the words were flashing and moving everywhere.

I didn't understand maths at all. On one occasion my teacher was shouting at me in front of the whole class. She said I couldn't go out at lunchtime until I'd learnt what we were doing and sent me away with a teaching assistant to go over it. She was so intimidating that, when I came back in, I'd forgotten what I'd learnt half way through. Luckily my friend was standing behind the teacher and she mouthed the answers to me.

When you don't understand something it makes you feel so upset in front of the whole class, especially when everyone else does understand. I felt like such an idiot. At least in secondary school we have different teachers. In primary you are stuck with the same teacher for the whole year and there are no lessons to look forward to.

When I was 12 our teacher told us in class that she was dyslexic. Afterwards, everyone started laughing about it. I felt so embarrassed because I knew that I was dyslexic too and it felt as if it was a bad thing to admit to. Only one of the girls there, a really good friend, knew about me because I had hidden it. She said to the others, 'Stop laughing because some girls here might have it', and they did stop.

I can still remember every detail of that moment to this day. I can remember exactly where we were and who was sitting where. I was trying to make the laugh everyone else was doing but no sound would come out of my mouth. Afterwards I couldn't thank my friend enough. She said to me, 'It's okay. It's going to be okay.'

Isla, 13, Lothian, Scotland

'Split smiley face with words.'

She's right. This year I started opening up. One of my friends is also dyslexic and she spoke to me about it and said it was nothing to be embarrassed about. She said we are all creative in our own ways and that there are lots of good things about being dyslexic.

I hadn't thought of it like this.

This friend is very motivational. She's taught me that it doesn't matter what anyone thinks of you. She's explained to me that lots of people who we look up to have dyslexia and they never stopped trying. There are great role models, including some of my teachers. If they can do what they have done, I can keep trying. I thought, 'I'm being scared for nothing.'

I knew that there were lots of people with dyslexia who had done well but I thought I wouldn't. I thought I would fail. When I started opening up to people I realised that my life could work out well too. An incredible relief.

I still find that work at school is really challenging. It can be overwhelming. You have to get on with it but it's so hard. Every single time it comes to a test I sit there and take a deep breath in. Sometimes I am so stressed I just can't do them at all. Tears come to my eyes. Everyone is writing away and I am panicking and thinking, 'By the time I stop panicking this test is going to be over.' Then my head starts hurting.

In the end I calm down and the test results aren't always bad.

The teachers say that if we don't pass our exams we aren't going to get anywhere. But one teacher told us, 'I came out of school with nothing. Look at where I am now.' I know school's very important but there are different ways of getting to where you want to be if you put in the effort.

I am worried about my exams but I am proud of myself that I have come this far. I used to be scared of asking questions in front of a class and I can do that now. It needs to be me who pushes myself to do this.

Last year one of the geography teachers told us to pick a city and write about it. I had written three lines. Everyone else had done pages. Afterwards the teacher had an outburst. She called me a 'sad soul' and said I couldn't read. I was fuming and thinking, 'How dare you say I can't read.' I never spoke to her again.

I do have a lot of empathy and I couldn't get my head round what she said. I kept thinking, 'How rude is that?' I would never say that to a child. You have your limits as to what you say as a teacher.

When I can't do something I get frustrated and overwhelmed very fast, but I am learning that just because the work looks hard doesn't mean I can't do it. I know it's important not to give up.

I can't wait to get out of school. I want to get an apprenticeship. Some people are more academic, some more creative. I'm creative in different ways. I'm a problem-solver. I like to help people.

We are all different kinds of people. You can feel like you are separate from everyone else but it is also good to be different.

I have let dyslexia hold me back a lot, but it is me. I am learning to accept myself.

Emma, 9, Buckinghamshire, England

One good thing about having dyslexia is that I have an understanding about how it feels for others if they are finding something hard. I notice if people are struggling.

I have great friends and that is really important to me. If I sit next to someone and they find something difficult I will normally help them because I know how annoying it is when you don't understand.

It's a bit frustrating when I'm reading and I miss out some words. Or I read a word and I mistake it for another word. Or I'm reading a book and I am too focused on the reading and so I don't take in the story. It can be annoying that the teachers keep thinking that they need to help you loads. You get lots of help when you just want to be left to do what you are doing.

This year I was assessed and told I have dyslexia. I didn't know what it meant but I knew I was finding stuff harder than other children in my class. Now I can see I need to work on certain areas. I'm getting a bit better but find spelling hard. I rush my sentences and miss out words, though I am good at having ideas and getting them down. Maths is hard. Decimals are hard.

I'm not very organised. Sometimes I get distracted really easily and I get told, 'You need to concentrate.' I can get lost in my imagination. Then I realise I have to find where we are and concentrate on what I'm supposed to be doing.

A close friend of mine is dyslexic. She's good at some things I'm not good at. I'm good at some things she's not good at, so we match and can help each other.

Jamie, 12, Glasgow, Scotland

I didn't mind the dyslexia at first. I was a bit slow at writing and I found spelling and reading difficult, though I'm really good at maths.

Then I proper started to struggle because there was a lot of writing, a lot of copying stuff off the board a lot of the time. I didn't finish it and I still don't finish.

I went to my pastoral care at school and I did a lot of tests. They sent an email to my teachers telling them I was dyslexic. Now I get extra time and a scribe.

Sometimes I get frustrated when I don't understand things. I've found out that the way I learn is really simple. It's through drawing. A lot of young people like to draw and a lot of people like to learn like that. It helps me take in information. I say instead of writing, draw – because it makes a mass of difference. Extra time in exams also really helps.

One of the things I'm good at is building relationships with people. I am a volunteer for DRC Generations, an organisation that teaches children to avoid drug, alcohol and tobacco misuse. I was taught in primary school by one of their volunteers and wanted to carry on myself.

The reason I started volunteering was because I got involved in some stuff that I shouldn't have been doing. I was being cheeky, hanging about with the wrong people. I decided I wanted to do something different.

I especially like teaching young people with dyslexia and autism, and finding creative ways to explain things to them. I like going into primary schools and youth groups and I think it works well because we are people not a lot older than the people we are teaching.

I want to be a primary teacher. I think doing a lot of voluntary work will help me. I'm part of a youth committee that makes improvements. I went to the City Chambers in Glasgow with some of the adults I work with who have learning difficulties and we won a special award for work in the west of Glasgow. Seeing their faces made me feel great. They can't read or write but I show them how to draw. They learn new skills through me. They love it.

One of the women I work with couldn't read or write. She went through school not being able to learn. Now I am teaching her so that she can read books to her grandchildren. I get help for my dyslexia and then I pass help on to her.

My friends think it's good that I do so much. A lot of them play football; some stay in their houses and play on their computers. I'm the only one out of all my friends who's doing all this voluntary work.

I don't think I would have stayed on for so long here if we didn't work so well together. We all support each other. I know what it's like to struggle and I want to help other people who are struggling.

──── #3 ────
Gaining role models

'Because Keira Knightley and Orlando Bloom
are successful, I knew I could be too.'

Amelia, 12, Victoria, Canada

What made me feel better about being dyslexic was hearing about the other people with dyslexia who were really successful, like Keira Knightley and Orlando Bloom from *Pirates of the Caribbean*. Because I knew they were successful, I knew I could be too.

I've heard that a high percentage of actors and actresses have dyslexia. I am pleased I am dyslexic because I'm not sure I would be an actor if I wasn't. I'm not so happy about dyslexia when I am doing math and all of that.

When I was about seven I started acting. Acting made me feel better about myself, more confident and happy. I have fun doing it, though learning lines is a real challenge. My coach makes me sing and dance the lines I need to remember, and that works well.

I also like drawing and song writing. I rap and make up my own songs and play them on a piano. Right now I'm writing my own screenplay. At school we had to write a story and I immediately wanted to change it into a movie. It's a Halloween story and it's scary. I don't check the spelling until after I'm done. I find hard words difficult to spell. I know when I have spelled something wrong but I don't know what the spelling should be. It's easier when I'm typing on the computer because there is a spell check.

I think my mom sort of knew I was dyslexic when I was four. I had difficulties learning names of colours and I would flip sounds round in words: for 'complicated' I would say 'comclipated'.

The hard things for me are math, spelling and phonics. I have trouble with them and with remembering things by rote. The others in my class would remember a list and say, 'I just did this and that and that and that and that', and I would only remember the last thing. I was slower at finishing schoolwork than them. I find it harder to process information to my brain when I'm really tired.

Homework-wise things are hard. It's my worst time and it's a struggle. I'd rather do homework at school because I can concentrate better and I'm not so tired. I get assistance to help me read some of the questions but I prefer to read the questions to myself – for some reason it's harder if someone else is reading them.

One of the reasons homework is hard is because I'm putting so much effort into other things. Sometimes I cry

Amelia, 12, Victoria, Canada

because I want to focus on my out-of-school activities. My coaching for auditions sometimes takes six or seven hours a week, but I love it. My favourite part was a murder mystery on TV when I had to eat ice cream until I felt sick. I got to do a short film recently, and I was in *Little Shop of Horrors* in the theatre and I got eaten by a plant! I have also done stunt work and got to fly on a wire.

It's hard when they come to you on the day of an audition and change the lines. Other times they don't give you the lines ahead of time. I have had parts in auditions where I have forgotten the lines. It's much easier now, but I still have to work. My coach and I discuss each piece and the character and motivation. It all helps me to remember. It's good to get feedback from the directors and casting agents. They say I did great and that I have potential.

Isobel, 17, Vale of Glamorgan, Wales

The best thing for me about being dyslexic is my mum's spirit. She's such a positive person and that is such a powerful influence on me. She was dyslexic as well, but no one picked it up; no one knew what was going on. She was frustrated and dropped marks because of her spelling. Teachers said it was because she was lazy. Finally, when she was doing her PhD, she was screened and they found out.

My mum has shown me that you may not be good at spelling but that doesn't affect how much you can contribute. At my last school my friend and I were on the debating team so dyslexia doesn't mean you can't think quickly. Ideas are

what's important – not the ability to remember a sequence
of letters. If you find a way to deal with global warming or
clean out the oceans, no one will say, 'I'm not listening
because the spelling is wrong.'

In our house we have always been positive about dyslexia.
We've never joked about it – you know those really stupid
jokes: 'A dyslexic walks into a bra...'

When I was younger I wasn't
very inspired in class. I didn't enjoy
reading much and I wasn't that
confident. It took an academic
year to get me the extra time. I had
extra lessons in school when I was
a lot younger and sorted out my
confusion about 'bs' and 'ds'.

> If you find a way
> to deal with global
> warming or clean
> out the oceans, no
> one will say, 'I'm not
> listening because the
> spelling is wrong.'

I think testing for dyslexia should be free. I'm really
sure one of my friends is dyslexic but her parents can't afford
the test.

To help with my handwriting, when I was six or seven my
mum and teacher created a history folder for me. I would
research different bits of history and then write about them.
It was something I really enjoyed and it helped a lot. For
maths, I took very detailed notes and annotated everything,
making sure everything was colour coded. I found it stressful
if my notes were unclear.

I find it nearly impossible to remember everything I need
to do or write down if the instructions have been given
orally. Taking notes is absolutely essential. I've also found that
when learning a language and learning to conjugate verbs it

helps to be given the information as soon as possible. Then I can look for the themes and patterns instead of having to memorise the tables individually.

I need to work harder than other people: I get extra time in exams but no extra time to learn the course.

On the whole, dyslexic is just something I am. It's both a positive and a negative. The negatives are that I do find language learning a little more difficult. The positives include all sorts of things I learn that I didn't know anything about when I put the wrong spellings into Google!

I feel frustrated because I am doing the International Baccalaureate. For English I'm at the highest grade possible now, but I have to work so much harder on Maths and Spanish. I have always found languages much harder. I've also found that I have had better ideas than anyone else and am just not able to spell them. I've decided that, as long as what I write is legible and easy to understand, a few letters in the wrong place will be okay.

Dyslexia is seen as a negative thing but I have seen pictures of people who were dyslexic and successful – like Churchill. This shows it's not a decisive factor in what you are going to achieve or how much you can achieve.

Kyla, 9, Ohio, USA

I know a lot of people who have dyslexia are famous artists and I really like that because I'm really good at art. I like to draw myself and fairies and rainbows and unicorns. A lot of stuff. I like using pencils rather than paint because it's easier to get all the detail in. When I'm older I'd like to be a painting and drawing artist. My mom has read me out lists of people who have dyslexia who have done very well.

Kyla, 9, Ohio, USA
'Kyla's art place.'

As well as art I like acting and making up stories. I have done some plays and I'm good at that. When I act I feel what kind of character I am. It can be difficult to learn my lines when I do plays. It's hard because I'm bad at memorising but I just practice every day. Sometimes acting helps me feel more confident but sometimes in my acting class I get a little shy in front of people.

I don't really like school much because it's really hard. There are about three people in my class who struggle and we all go to a different teacher rather than stay in our class. She teaches us spelling and reading most of the time. We play games with her and that helps us learn.

When we have partners for reading I find some people don't like being my partner because I don't read fast. I don't really like that. They are not mean to me but I still don't like it.

The worst thing a teacher can do is not help me when I need it. In second grade I would say to the teacher a lot of times I needed help and she would say, 'Ask a neighbour', but they don't really like to help me because I ask them every day. I would help a child with dyslexia. I thought I was stupid and finding out I was dyslexic was a relief to me. It showed me there was a reason things were hard. I told my classmates and became more confident. I am much happier now.

My dyslexic Idol is....

....Leonardo DaVinci!

Dylan, 10, Cardiff, Wales
'My dyslexic idol.'

#4
Being different

'I can't imagine not seeing things differently.'

Lucy, 11, Bay of Plenty, New Zealand

I have always wanted to be the president of New Zealand. If I was the president I would help kids with dyslexia and I would buy each of them a horse. When you're with horses you don't have to think about schoolwork. With animals you can just enjoy yourself.

They will have to pay for their own food for the horses though.

Horses are cool. They smell great, they are very elegant and they are fun to ride. We have a horse outside where we live that belongs to our neighbour and also highland cattle grazing outside so I get to look at all of them.

I'm a creative person with a very active mind. This is good but it makes it harder to fall asleep at night. I think about everything: horses – because my mum and dad bought me some horse-riding lessons for my birthday; my day at school;

53

cockroaches – because I hate cockroaches and when I think of them I have to turn the light on to make sure there are none in my room. We live near lots of farmland so there are lots of cockroaches in the area.

Even though I have dyslexia it doesn't stop me from jumping for my dreams!

Amelia, 10, Cardiff, Wales

When I am older I have wanted to be a zookeeper, a vet, a famous horse rider, a horse trainer, a person who owns a ranch – and also a nail stylist and hairdresser.

When I was younger reading made me feel seasick, really ill. I could see the white bits more than the black bits, but I still felt that I was doing fine. I can't spell – sometimes I forget how to spell 'then'. Maths is better than my spelling and my reading, but division is really hard.

Now I am in intermediate school the work is harder and I notice that I find things a lot more difficult. When I ask something in class the others might say, 'I thought you knew how to spell that', and laugh. I'm used to people laughing at me. It's a thing that happens a lot in my family, in a good way. I get laughed at a lot at school because they find me funny so I take it as they are laughing at me because I am funny, not because they want to be mean. I know they think I'm smart.

Rachel, 11, London, England

The best thing about dyslexia is that it makes me more curious about things. It means I am more forgetful but also more able to picture things. It's good for my imagination. If I have to write a story I am good at thinking up the details. It may be hard for me to write it but I can picture it in my head. I can see it and smell it.

Sometimes when teachers say something and ask a question it makes me think of a question back. Then I think of another question for their answer, then another one. Sometimes the teachers say to me, 'I can't think of an answer but I will try to look it up.' If they do answer it, I picture what they are saying. It's like I'm painting a picture in my mind.

I use images in my head to remember things. Say me and mum are going shopping and might forget to bring the list, I picture the list and know what to buy. I have to write a list for school so I don't forget anything and when it's written I picture the list to put it in my head.

When I'm about to leave for school I picture myself at school. I have to wear a lanyard and it's hard to remember it, so I picture what I need to be wearing and then I remember the lanyard. I picture things in 3D, not flat. I like making things visual so I can remember them.

Elspeth, 10, Perthshire, Scotland
'When the person has got dyslexia in my picture she takes the winding road. It takes her longer but she gets more ideas that way. The person who has not got dyslexia is quicker but she doesn't get as many ideas.'

When I had my dyslexia test, the person who gave it to me asked me a question. 'Here is a rubber and here is some paper. What is the link between the two?' I said the link was trees because they both come from trees. The person said most people would say that a pencil is what links them because I have to write with one on the paper and rub out any mistakes. I was pleased my answer was a bit different.

I think I spell in an interesting way too. I don't think my spelling is wrong. I think I just spell differently to the way other people spell. I thought dyslexia was spelt 'dislexer' because when you say dyslexia you wouldn't think there was a 'y'. You would think there was an 'i'.

Helena, 18, London, England

When a teacher asks me a question, I can tell that I'm thinking about the answer in a different way from other people. I think about things from a different viewpoint. Sometimes the teachers say, 'That's an unusual way of seeing it.'

Everyone thinks there is one way of dealing with a problem, but I will have a different perspective. If someone pulled a gun on you, someone with dyslexia will think about the situation in a completely different way. It could save my life!

> If I'm on a bus and I see someone walking down the street I will suddenly have a whole storyline in my head...

If I'm on a bus and I see someone walking down the street I will suddenly have a whole storyline in my head and know how the film would be shot, the colours in it. The whole thing.

I have never said to myself I wish I didn't have dyslexia. I have just accepted it. I didn't struggle that badly at school. I think the reason I don't struggle is that I enjoy the subjects, though I can get stuck on what the question is really asking me.

In Maths I normally get to an answer really quickly. It just makes a lot of sense. Sometimes on an exam paper I can't do the easy questions but I can do the harder ones.

Helena, 18, London, England

At times I'm reading and I'm half way down the page and I realise I haven't been reading at all. I skip lines easily. I see certain letters and think it's saying a particular word and it isn't that word at all. I always think about the outcome while I'm reading and this means I don't quite get there.

Sometimes when I was young I stepped away from trying at something because I knew I was dyslexic. Even now if I know I won't get to the answer I don't want to try.

Cole, 8, Illinois, USA

I like being different and, as much as people with dyslexia have difficulties, we also have strengths. Maybe if I wasn't dyslexic I would just be average at everything. One of my

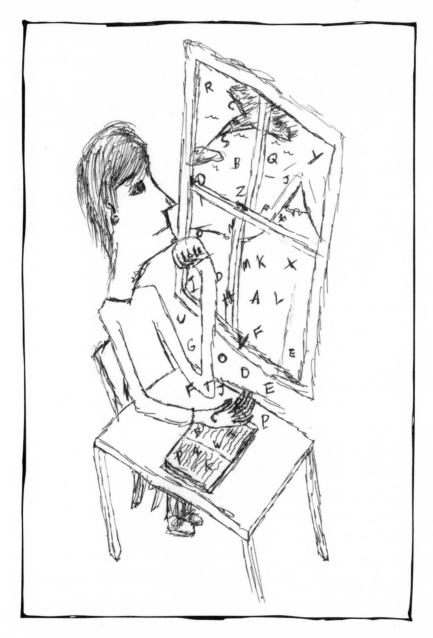

Conor, 15, London, England

'I think that daydreaming is like falling into my imagination without having to think about anything else.'

strengths is writing. I'm bad at reading but really good at writing.

I write scary stories, funny stories and problem-solving stories. In school right now I'm writing about how two friends got into an argument, how they said they were not friends any more and how the parents are trying to help. Sometimes I wake up at night because I have a new story in my mind. I have all these ideas for stories shooting round my head.

> # The News
>
> a nice, generous kid named, Cole Svara, has turned into a beast. They are saying that he turned into a beast because, school was too hard for him because of dyslexia. Dyslexia makes kids have a disadvantage.

Cole, 8, Illinois, USA
'The News.'

In my classroom I wrote a spooky story. It was about me and my mom. We were sitting on the couch at home and we heard a noise behind us. We both turned back and after we turned to the front again I looked and my mom wasn't there. Instead I saw a black shape and it started chasing me. I ran to my room and turned on the light and I heard, 'Boo.' Everyone was there – all my friends were round for a surprise party. I asked them, 'Where's my mom? Who took my mom? Someone took her, someone in a black cloak. He was chasing me up the stairs.' They didn't believe me but then they saw him. Scary!

Cole, 8, Illinois, USA
'Turning into a monster.'

I think I'm also good at art, sports and math. I'm one of the best math students in my whole class. My spelling is good now. I go to a tutor and she helped me a lot. Before I this I couldn't read or sound out all the small words. I like reading big print but now I'm getting better and that's good because the only books that have big, bold words are children's baby books. Now we read books for older kids and my mom reads a page and I read a page. If my mom didn't help me and get me tested for dyslexia in the first place I would still be reading baby books. It's just getting the words off the page – that's what I have to do.

> **I have all these ideas for stories shooting round my head.**

Once I started going to the tutor I was writing more right away. It's just me and her. If there were other students it would take more time and I would get confused. She would be working with me one second and then working with him then back to me. I would forget what we were doing and have to ask, 'How do you sound this out again?'

Samuel, 12, New Brunswick, Canada

I know I'm skilled at thinking differently. Definitely my mind works in another way from other people. I play sports pretty good. I play defence in American football, trying to tackle the people running with the ball. Some people might think I'm going to put in this pass but I'll do something different.

If I see a car being fixed using machines I think, 'Why rely on machines and new technology?' I question things: 'Why not do it this way, with your hands?' They can do this one way, I can do this two ways. If you are going to tackle this guy, find another way. Don't have all ten people on one guy to tackle him. Spread out. Have new ideas.

Some of my ideas are straightforward. I want to go into the military, into the ground forces or maybe be a military police officer. My grampy was in the military as a chief warrant officer. My great grampy was in World War 2. My uncle went to Afghanistan multiple times. I want to serve my country and help people to feel safe. I am proud of them and want to carry on this tradition.

If you have a best friend you can tell them about your dyslexia but you don't have to tell everyone else. You can just say, 'I learn differently from other people.' You don't have to say you learn the dyslexic way. Sometimes they might not know what it means and you don't have to explain it to them.

If people try to tease you, you can just ignore them. Maybe yours is the right way to learn.

Social Studies, Science, French, English, Math – I don't like any of it. I know it's important but I find it really tough. I found out I was dyslexic a year ago. I had found writing and trying to learn difficult. Sometimes I'd get really frustrated. I couldn't understand what they were trying to teach.

Mom and Dad would have to have meetings with teachers. Then I went to a professional for tests. They told me I was dyslexic but I didn't know what it meant.

Now I learn things in a different way. I use a computer at school or an iPad or if I'm doing a test the teacher reads the questions out to me. Even now, everything I'm doing in class is not really fun. I'm just sitting there when I could be outside and having fun with my friends.

Sometimes I take a break from class and walk around the school and refresh. Getting a drink can help. Being around my family helps too, them supporting me. Try your best and that's all you can do and hopefully everybody will like it. If people try to say you have a disability or want to exclude you I would just say, 'I'm a normal kid. I learn different from you; you learn differently from me.'

Gabriella, 17, Gibraltar

The way I think – it's just me. I have my imagination. I see things the way others don't. If I wasn't dyslexic I wouldn't see the world the way I see it; everything would have been so much plainer. With dyslexia life is so much more colourful.

I have a childish mindset. When other people are down or getting stressed I think, 'I'm going to forget that. It's a beautiful day. Why don't I just be happy with that.' I think of something else and get lost in my imagination. When I'm with animals it's almost as if the animals talk to me. Everything seems so simple and easier to understand than learning normal subjects. Animals are in 3D. This helps because you can see them in your head and in your eyes.

Eventually I'd like to work with exotics like big cats, on vaccines or their immune systems. I have a passion for biology and science and love endangered animals.

At school I put in so much effort, I felt as if I was drowning in the work, trying to keep up. At times I felt, 'What's the point of doing it if it's not going to get better?' But it does get better and when you've done the exams everything disappears, all the worries and everything.

I found out I was dyslexic when I was nine or ten. I was moving schools and had to do a test. Because I had a big learning gap they thought they would put me down a year but then they decided they wouldn't and put me in my correct year. They told my mum the learning gap was so big I didn't know what I should have known for the year below.

> It's so important not to give up just because your English and Maths is getting you down. These are just two subjects.

I worked so hard and my GCSEs were a good enough standard for A levels but I decided to go down the BTEC [Business and Technology Education Council] route. I preferred the way they were taught – in a more practical way. Now I'm studying animal management. It's so important if you have dyslexia to find something you are passionate about in school or outside of it: something you can build on, learn about and have fun with. It really does help. It's so important not to give up just because your English and Maths is getting you down. These are just two subjects. We with dyslexia are stronger in other areas.

Rocco, 11, Hertfordshire, England

The black bits in my drawing are the bad things about having dyslexia and the white bits are what's good. The bad bits are the slow writing and the slow reading and forgetting things, including spellings and leaving things at home or at school.

The good thing about having dyslexia is thinking differently. Sometimes I work out maths questions differently from other people.

Rocco, 11, Hertfordshire, England
'Good and bad things about being dyslexic.'

When I was ten I knew I was dyslexic. I did an assessment test. I sort of felt sad and a tiny bit happy. I thought that it made sense. The teachers act like dyslexia is a 'big thing' and that's a bit annoying, but I can understand my schoolwork a bit better. I get annoyed that my younger brother is doing better in school than me but, in a way, when you're trying your best you can just forget that you have it.

My teacher told me that he had a bit of a confession — he is dyslexic too. He tells me to write things on Post-it notes to help me remember.

I like to play electric guitar. I used to practise the acoustic guitar but moved on to electric. My music teacher says I'm very good at listening to the notes rather than reading them on paper. Sometimes I record songs. My guitar teacher is in a band and writes his own music and I would like to do that too.

When I'm older I know I want to do something that gets paid quite a bit. I have liked story writing since I was very young. At the moment I have a book in my head called *Ezdo*. The hero has to find a sword and on the way he finds these magical creatures. He tames a golden eagle queen and she helps him from that point on. He finds the sword and he gets trapped in the labyrinth. The minotaur traps him, and the eagle queen uses the sword to defeat the minotaur. I have just been planning the book but I'm going to write it down. I like drawing mythical creatures too, like the phoenix.

I have another idea — about a boy who gets dropped on a Monopoly board and has to make his way around it. I have too many ideas and I'm scared that I will forget them, so once I've finished one book I will start on the next.

Veronica, 14, London, England

I'm good at art, drawing and noticing all the little details in between what is drawn. When I was five my brother had to paint something and I noticed all the little strokes. It's as if I can see things that no one else really sees.

I put my creative skills down to being dyslexic and seeing things differently, seeing things in such detail. I will remember where I put the house keys because I will picture them. Colours help me a lot at school and I use highlighters.

The best thing is probably knowing there are different sides to dyslexia. I can't imagine not seeing things differently, knowing there are so many people with the same thing and so many successful people have it. My mum started crying when she found out – there's a lot of negative pressure on people. I said, 'If so many other successful people are dyslexic, why can't I be the same?' If other people can do it so can I.

When I found out I had dyslexia, my teacher told me it was a learning disability and I said, 'Disability is like a wheelchair. I would rather you say "learning difference".' She just looked at me and smiled.

At 10 or 11 I had read all of the Harry Potter books so for me reading is not the problem, writing is the issue. I have many ideas and creatively it's getting the ideas from my head to my arm to the paper. They disappear on the way. It just doesn't work. I have struggled a lot in writing and spelling. I couldn't differentiate between 'there', 'their' and 'they're'. I couldn't spell 'because' until last year.

> ...my teacher told me it was a learning disability and I said, 'Disability is like a wheelchair. I would rather you say "learning difference".'

My handwriting is dreadful because my brain works faster than my arm. I would miss out words because I wanted to get to the point. Everyone else would be getting the gold stars and I would get the stamp saying, 'Try to improve on this.'

As for my memory, I remember certain things. I can remember exactly what the rubbish bin in my Year 6 classroom looked like but I can't remember the teacher's name.

When you find out you're dyslexic a weight is lifted off your shoulders because you know you're not weird. However, a different weight is put on there. I had to prove to people that it's

> It's getting the ideas from my head to my arm to the paper. They disappear on the way.

not that bad. People presume you can't read well but we had reading tests two years ago and everyone got either aged 11 or 12 in reading and my result was 16 plus.

Corey, 10, Vale of Glamorgan, Wales

Since I have come to terms with dyslexia, the best thing is knowing. I'd say to anyone go and get the test. With my older brother they just thought he wasn't paying attention. After GCSEs he found out he was pretty badly dyslexic. From then to now there's been a big difference in the way dyslexia is seen. A lot of people may be ashamed of dyslexia but there are so many people in a similar position and so many successful people who are dyslexic.

Henry, 13, County Carlow, Ireland

Generally when people hear the words, 'I'm dyslexic', they label you as being stupid or less intelligent but I don't like that. It doesn't represent what dyslexic is. To me, dyslexia is just the extra creativity. That's the main focus. I like to draw; I like to create things. I do a lot of drawing and a lot of craft projects in whatever space I can find.

> There are a couple of people I admire, including Steve Wozniak who is the co-founder of Apple. I think he's a bit underappreciated.

Dyslexia doesn't really limit me that much and there are a lot of benefits. It's great when I get to solve a problem or make a decision. People have said to me I work out puzzles very quickly.

I have always been told I was dyslexic. I always knew that was the reason I was being helped.

I really enjoy all my subjects. I'm not able to do a language so I don't learn Gaelic and haven't since I was five or six. So when the others are learning Irish [Gaelic] I go to a room and do my homework. My friends know what dyslexia is and perfectly understand why I'm not in the class.

Henry, 13, County Carlow, Ireland

When I had learning support when I was young the teacher talked to me like I was a child and I didn't like that. When I said I was okay with a subject or okay with a concept they still pressed on, trying to teach it to me, even when I got a high score. She would still have to go through the whole thing because she was following something given to her by the Board of Education. That was annoying.

I have had some help with spelling. The ones I have trouble with are the sort of words you don't use in everyday sentences, like 'quiche', that use a lot of small-sounding vowels and letters. Maths is good. Art is very good.

I'm not sure what I want to do when I'm older. I think I'd like to start a business. I like the idea of having something that you control and that allows you to make decisions.

Because of this I would like to study some kind of business studies. I don't look up to any particular person but there are a couple of people I admire, including Steve Wozniak who is the co-founder of Apple. I think he's a bit underappreciated.

David, 12, County Offaly, Ireland

The best thing about dyslexia is that you are different. I don't mind being different. Usually I don't let it bother me. Sometimes I'm sad. Sometimes I wonder about secondary school and what it will be like.

I knew I was dyslexic when I was ten. Maths gets hard and so does spelling and reading. I wasn't doing as well as the others. I felt a little bit like I wish I could just keep up.

Then one of the teachers talked to me and Mammy and I got assessed. Now I feel like I'm different – in a good way. My brain works differently from other people. Sometimes if I do maths and I'm stuck on a sum I do tricks that some of the teachers taught me. I have 100 squares and use them to help work out answers. They also gave me coloured paper and that helps.

I started playing golf two years ago. Playing golf is an escape for me. I like being outside and feeling calm and no one disturbing me. I achieve a new task with every hole. I love hitting the ball far and in the right direction. The golfer Shane Lowry is from our town and his dad Brendan has offered for me to play on different courses with him this year. I would like that to be my job. Or I would like to be an archaeologist, finding bones. I am aiming very high in my career. I love that Jamie Oliver is dyslexic.

Sometimes it's the way I learn that makes a difference. I prefer hearing something to reading or writing it. I don't like reading a lot but it has to be done. I prefer someone else to read to me. I am confident in different things. My mammy tries to give me stuff to do outside school so I don't feel down.

Fiona, 15, Bedfordshire, England

When I'm playing netball I can stand back and read the game and help the others by telling them where the ball's going. In hockey I'm more in the middle of it but I can read the game then too.

I actually like maths. I like getting through it slowly and problem-solving. What I like is that there's not just one way to answer a question. If I can't do something I can get there another way.

On the other hand, my dad who is dyslexic sees how I spell words, and says, 'That's how I spell it', and my mum and two sisters say, 'No, that's really wrong.' So thinking differently is not always useful!

I found out I had dyslexia in Year 6 when I was 11 and it felt like I was spelling everything wrong. I would be taking spelling tests and I would revise them and revise them and would still get five or six out of ten.

My Year 6 teacher said I should be tested for dyslexia. I didn't really understand what it was but I was confused about why I couldn't do the spellings and the rest of the class could. I was always the lowest.

When I came to secondary school I started getting academic support. We did spelling and tests and that helped a lot. Now the support is more for improving my organisational skills and helping me to revise. I used to be really, really disorganised. I'd forget everything. I would forget my pencil case and my planner or to get my planner signed. I still can't really remember much but I'm getting better. I now have ways of remembering things. I write the instruction down as soon as I'm told to do something. My dad didn't ever get any help. He forgets everything.

I'm interested in sports and art and design technology. I think I'm more creative because I knew I wasn't good at English and Science so I tried to find different subjects. I think I've realised that dyslexia doesn't make that much difference. If I work hard I feel the same as everyone else. I try really hard and then try harder and revise more.

Ella, 11, Manchester, England

Learning about animals is much easier for me than learning about spellings and maths. When I'm doing this I feel as if I am in the place I should be.

I have always had a soft spot for animals. I always liked them more than most other things. Animals can't spell so in a way they are dyslexic as well. When you learn about animals you don't have to read. You can put on a video, or someone can tell you about them, or you can look after them. That's all you need to do to put animals into context.

I learn about animals mostly out of school. On YouTube some films are cute but others are educational like *Planet Earth*. Some people make money and get quite rich making films. I think that kind of work would be great, like being another David Attenborough.

Art is an advantage for me and I really like drawing animals. At home I have a cat whose name is Silky and I can draw quite good cats. I like painting too. Sometimes I'm good at listening and I'm good at understanding. Being dyslexic does have quite a lot of advantages.

> Animals can't spell so in a way they are dyslexic as well.

Dyslexia does make me a bit different from everyone else. My friends have helped me quite a lot, because they are really kind. They tell me to ignore bullies and people teasing me. This makes me feel less alone. My parents have helped me too. They are dyslexic and I must have inherited it.

I find spelling is really difficult and maths is quite difficult as well. Mostly spelling. Mostly grammar! School can be really hard, especially in Maths, trying to work out a sum and feeling like everyone else can do it and I can't.

I remember in Year 5 we had to do spellings and if we didn't get them all right we had to stay in until we did. I started off with zero right and I ended up doing them ten times. This meant 100 spellings and that wasn't exactly fun.

Ryan, 9, Colorado, USA

I found out I was dyslexic three years ago. I couldn't remember whether an 'a' was an 'a' or a 'b' was a 'b'. It felt weird that I couldn't learn the words. My mom tried flash cards and some apps on her phone. They didn't really help.

I didn't want to go to school and I cried about it a lot. I remember telling my mom that my stomach hurt. It felt like I always had to read these boring stories that didn't make any sense. I had some trouble understanding them.

Some of my friends know I have dyslexia but I don't talk about it at school. It does make me sad when we have to read our papers to the class or when other kids read my paper. One kid told me I need to practise more. I felt bad about that.

When I read I often get the word wrong, but somehow the word still makes sense in the sentence. So, when I read it's almost like I know what the sentence says without reading all of the words. This doesn't always work and this can lead to mistakes, especially with math word problems.

The best thing about being dyslexic is that I'm special because not everybody has this. I do things differently. The teacher gives us a problem and I will always work it out differently.

The worst thing a teacher can do is go too fast. The best thing is to go slow and make sure everybody understands what they are saying. My mom helps me most. She teaches me spelling. She makes me do the work, but she helps me break it down one step at a time.

Lola, 18, London, England
'My school day.'

I am good at math. I'm good at making friends and I'm good at making things. I make whatever I want to make. I just taught myself how to make Rainbow Loom snakes. I like just putting stuff together. I have made a travel pillow backpack before. I want to be an architect when I am older. I love skyscrapers and I would like to design them.

Miles, 13, Victoria, Australia

Everyone says people with dyslexia think in different ways. That could be true. My grandparents live near a place where you can shape gemstones. We talked to them and asked if I could join. I shape the stones using big industrial machinery.

There are different levels of hardness with stones. You have to learn how to work on each of them. I like soft stones like jade and opals. The organisation supplies the jewellery and I make the stones that are used in it. This year I came third in the first gem competition I went in for.

When I leave school I want to be a gemmologist, someone who works with gemstones. This is like a geologist but one who focuses much more than on stones and rocks. There are lots of opals here in Australia. The lightning opals are the ones people want most, so sometimes they throw out the ordinary opals and I can work on them. I like to collect them and one day I would like to turn them into 'cabochons', or polished gems, and exhibit them. Opals are very fragile and break easily. You need lots of experience to work with them.

I think it's a great idea for someone with dyslexia to find a hobby outside of school and get some friends to do it with you. If you can do that you will be a lot happier.

A lot of people say that people with dyslexia think outside of the box. If someone has a problem everyone else might see it in one way. I would see it completely differently to other people, in a way no one else has thought about. That gives me a different perspective.

At first I didn't go to the best school for helping with dyslexia. They taught me like everyone else. They had a certain way to do stuff and if you couldn't do that they would say go and work on it at home by yourself. They didn't explain it so I got further and further behind.

They would give you a fair amount of homework and it would take me a lot longer. So I wouldn't do my homework or I would be behind and then I wouldn't feel the best about it.

I wasn't exactly bullied. It was a 'self thing'. I would feel that I was a below average person. I didn't think I was stupid but I wasn't good at things I was doing in class so felt uncomfortable there.

Things got better for me when I switched school. Here they help more. I noticed when I got here that all the teachers are very friendly and know how to work with kids with dyslexia a lot more. I have had my Year 7 exams and they weren't that bad. I thought I would have done a lot worse.

Grace, 14, County Kildare, Ireland

I'd say to anyone with dyslexia not to worry because you will probably get on a lot better after school. Textbooks are not aimed at us. They weren't written for us and that makes it a lot harder for us to understand them. That's why kids with dyslexia don't do well in school. We are not prioritised.

I found out I was dyslexic when I was ten. I was confused about what it was, although I had been told. I talked to a few of my friends about it and they said I was special needs and that I had a learning difficulty. They said it meant that I wasn't as smart as anyone else. I was really upset. I don't think they meant to be mean: I don't think they understood it either.

I like to be able to talk about dyslexia now and I think that not that many people understand it. They think it means you can't read – and for me ten pages is a lot – but lots of other things are hard too. Remembering things is difficult.

When I was young and struggling with reading, writing, spelling and maths I thought everyone else was having the same problems. When you have dyslexia you have a waiver for learning Irish but I went to an all-Irish school where we weren't allowed to speak or write in English, and if we did we got into trouble.

I thought that I wasn't as good at learning as the others. I didn't know that the Irish was making it harder for me.

Now I'm in secondary school and I still do Irish. It wasn't worth learning it for eight years and then dropping it. I do go to an English school now. It would have been too hard to go on to an all-Irish secondary school.

I want to be a vet when I'm older, working in the outdoors, talking to different people and helping animals. I don't want to be indoors working in an office or on a computer. I think it would remind me of school.

In my first year of secondary school my maths teacher was really strict. She didn't like people who weren't able to keep up. If you didn't keep up she would forget you were there. If you asked her a question, she would say, 'Don't ask me', so it wouldn't be worth it. When teachers get annoyed because we are asking too many questions they say, 'Ask the people beside you', but they are the teacher. We should ask them. They also say, 'You should have been listening the first time.' Unfair.

They should try to understand where we're coming from, not ignore us. They should try their best to help us even if they don't understand what it's like to be dyslexic.

The best thing about dyslexia is probably that I'm not like everybody else. I like to be different. I have got dyspraxia as well. I go to a workshop on Mondays after school for two hours and we do English and Maths. I have been going for years. Sometimes I don't want to go – I don't want two more hours of school – but it does help me. Without it I would be a lot worse than I am.

5

Making me stronger

'I was a shell of a kid. You can see the growth in me.'

Phoebe, 10, Victoria, Australia

I am able to read people's expressions. If someone is upset I can tell without them saying anything and I can cheer them up. I think I'm good at noticing what other people are feeling because of what has happened to me.

At school I felt like I was the only one who was struggling. I wondered why the other kids could read better. I didn't tell mum about how I felt till later on when the bullying got worse. It started with just a little push every day and when I was older it started getting a little more violent and they would call me names and push me around and tease me. I thought it would make things better for me if I told them I had dyslexia – they were the first people I had told – but they started making fun of me. They said I was tall and weak and weird and they called me 'vacuum cleaner': someone who doesn't understand well and is dizzy and doesn't know what is going in.

Darcey, 8, Cardiff, Wales

The group got a little bit bigger but they were saying the same things: that I was dumb, I didn't know what I was talking about and that they didn't care that I was dyslexic. They kept pushing me around the playground and eventually I purposely went to sick bay to get away from them and the people at sick bay treated me very nicely.

Eventually I told my parents and we moved school. At this school there's just one boy who's just a tiny bit mean but he doesn't push or shove. Besides that I have lots of friends.

> When I cycle it's like I had been on a lead and then I have broken free and I'm my own person.

My mum and my dad have helped me get through the tough situations. Everything that happened to me does still affect me. I still get some memories of the girls who bullied me but, besides that, I think all that has happened has improved me. I am able to stand up for what's right. I know now I don't have to be so small. I don't have to let myself be pushed around. In that way it's made me a stronger person. This makes me feel I got bullied for a reason: to go to another school and stand up for what I think is right.

In my schoolwork I have most words under control and my memory for times tables is getting better. Spellings are most difficult for me. I can't spell really, really long words. Multi-syllable words? I can't even spell 'multi-syllable'!

There are other things that I'm good at. I have won six medals in bike riding, some for sprint and some for 100 km. I like that when I'm on my bike I can think back to when I got bullied and it moves me forward. When I cycle it's like I had been on a lead and then I have broken free and I'm my own person.

Dyslexia isn't a curse. It's a gift. It provides hope for you to live a better life so you can be whatever you want. If you want to be a writer, it won't stop you. I want to be an inventor. I want to invent a hover board that actually works. I want to invent a machine to help kids if they are in hospital, that can use technology that can help teach sick kids how to read and write.

Most people would think you have to use a switch to turn on a light but maybe that is not the only way. Maybe you could have a little bit of electricity in your fingertip and you can wave your hand in front of a sensor to make the lights go up or down, or on or off. Or maybe the light switch could sense you were about to touch it and that would be enough to change the lights in a room.

With dyslexia you can think in different ways. Everyone else is pink and we are yellow so we are really cool. We are different in the world.

Kaitlyn, 12, Victoria, Australia

I realised when I was around nine that something was wrong with me and I didn't like it. I found reading, writing, spelling and copying off the board hard and I was by myself a lot. I was usually sent outside to do my spellings with a teacher with a fairly strong accent and I didn't understand her. The lawnmower was mowing the grass at that time and I was there with two other kids and we couldn't hear.

The other people out there with me were people with behaviour problems. I didn't feel I fitted in with them either. They had decided not to do the work; I couldn't do it. The teacher would say I wasn't trying hard enough.

I used to hold on to my mum or dad as we were walking into school. It was like the movies: I would hold on to their leg and wouldn't let go. The class was quite chaotic, and background noise and distorted speech are a big problem for me.

One of my grade three teachers kept me in when everyone else had gone to lunch. She told me to cut out the crying because I was just being stupid. She said my family was disappointed in me because of it. She told me, 'There's nothing wrong with you, you're just lazy.'

I sat near the back door and if someone walked in I used to bolt out, and run away from school; climb a tree or hide in a bush. I remember once in the morning chasing my mum's car down to the main road after being dropped off. I didn't want her to go.

In grade five we moved house and I started at a different primary school. My teacher was really nice and my class was awesome. They taught the subjects differently, though, and because we had moved states and they all teach differently I missed chunks of my education.

When I was 11 I was diagnosed with dyslexia after my mum spotted it. The school made accommodations including audiobooks, teachers reading things to me, and not having to copy as much work down. There was more help. At first I was a bit embarrassed because I felt like the whole room was treating me as if I was the centre of attention. I thought the others were thinking, 'Why is she allowed to do that?' I didn't use everything I was allowed.

I use the accommodations a lot more now and they have improved things for me. It's great being able to type my assessments and being allowed to bring my iPad to school. The other kids have got used to it, though I asked in Humanities if I could use my phone for something and the others said, 'Why does she get to use her phone?'

It's good to remember the teachers who are kind. One teacher I had early on was awesome. I suffered from anxiety and she would meet me at the front gate and walk me to class every morning. My humanities teacher now comes straight to me if I have my hand up, I might ask her to re-read something so I can understand it better. My English teacher is really nice. It's great that the two subjects I struggle with the most have the two nicest teachers.

Mum has helped most. She's the one who's sat down and helped me with my homework. She talks with me when I'm upset and saying I can't do something. She's the person I always turn to.

Last year I did two class presentations about dyslexia. The first time I gave my talk I was scared but the second time I said to myself, 'What is the worst thing that can happen? They can block their ears.' One of the grade three classes sent letters to me afterwards saying, 'You're so brave to do this.' That was a very big boost of confidence.

I understand now that just because I don't have something they have, I also have something they don't have.

The best thing about dyslexia is all the bonus talents that come along with it. When we lived in Darwin I used to make little houses for the ants with water bottles. I made snail gardens and miniature models with miniature wooden sticks. People say I have a great imagination. I can see a pile of stuff and see the potential where most people just see rubbish.

> My mum told me that when you have a job you don't do tests every week and I can't believe that they will come to an end one day.

I know I want to work with animals when I'm older. I love animals because they don't judge you. There's a connection with dyslexia because, whenever I'm upset or don't really want to talk to anyone, I always have a little fluffy dog or guinea pig or chicken to talk to. They don't make you talk about things you don't want to talk about.

School isn't for your whole life. My mum told me that when you have a job you don't do tests every week and I can't believe that they will come to an end one day. The important thing is to follow something you love and turn it into a career.

Life does get better. It's a hill and at first you have to climb up before you can go back down. You are not alone. There will always be someone out there, at least one other person, who struggles the same way you do. And they will understand.

Abbie, 11, Aberdeenshire, Scotland

'I am proud to be dyslexic because now I know why I get things wrong. I only found out about a month ago and I have struggled for a long time.'

What changed for me? I stopped looking at what goes wrong and started looking at what could go right. I had been like some fugitive trying to hide and dyslexia was the cops. It had taken a lot of effort pretending I could understand what other people were reading. I stopped hiding and started being proud of who I am. I found a support group and got to meet other people with dyslexia, a room of good people who understood me and who knew what I might need to help me.

Every time I go to class or school people start to understand me a little bit more. I have close friends. Before I wasn't so close to people so I couldn't tell them I was struggling.

I think dyslexia has made me a stronger person. I started looking up and it felt so much easier than being down every second of the day. I feel like I'm actually alive. I'm looking up to the sky.

Jordan, 14, London, England

I had been struggling at school and I thought I wasn't working hard enough. Then I went for a few assessments and they said I was dyslexic and my problems at school weren't my fault. This has helped me because now people get why I don't understand particular things or why they take me longer. They used to put it down to me not concentrating and this made me frustrated and I tuned out. Now I know it's not me and I stay calm.

I find reading, writing and spelling difficult. My maths is all right. I don't struggle as much when I read now because I read every day. I like crime books. Reading is something I had talked myself into not liking. I think I probably did always like reading but I didn't do it because I didn't know how to do it properly.

I like different things. I like colours; I like things to have order; I like facts. I like physics because you can see the evidence. I like working out why one person's wrong and the other person's right. When I leave school I think I want to be a child psychologist or a lawyer or be in the army.

> I feel as if I have overcome something and not everyone has had that experience so I feel better for that.

When I think about dyslexia I think that anybody could have it. It's unseeable. It's not just that you're different – it's that you're not the same. I feel as if I have overcome something and not everyone has had that experience so I feel better for that. Fighting for things shows you can do them.

Katelynn, 15, Michigan, USA

In first grade, homework that should have taken me five or ten minutes took an hour. I felt I was slower than everyone else in reading and writing. I thought this was just me. I got bullied quite a bit and I would cry at home and not want to go to school. I had headaches and stomach aches and a lot of anxiety. The girls were materialistic and cliquey and they would exclude anyone who was different.

My mom bought me the book *Fish in a Tree* and I fell in love with it. I thought that the teachers and other kids should know what kids with dyslexia were struggling with on a daily basis. I decided to do a presentation at school about dyslexia as one of the projects for my confirmation classes for church.

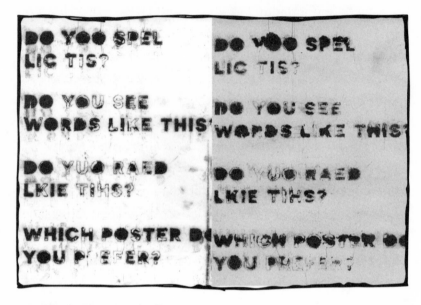

Daisy, 17, Somerset, England
'How words look to me.'

I found out that I had a knack for public speaking and the staff said, 'Good job.' They really didn't know all these things. They had questions and I had some answers. This was a changing moment for me and made me feel stronger. I have since moved on to high school and I spoke to the high school staff. Teachers there were engaged and interested too.

I'm not worried what anyone thinks of me when I talk to teachers or students. I just want to make myself heard. I was invited to speak at another elementary school where the principal wanted to do something about dyslexia so students wouldn't dislike school.

The teachers were interested in the struggle I've had so they can help other students. Some wondered who else they may have missed along the way. Presenting to people about dyslexia makes me feel proud of who I am. It makes me feel strong and alive. In fact I've realised that I want to be a teacher when I am older.

There still are difficult times. There is still some bullying but I have learned to forgive them. I have learned to ignore them when they tell me I can't be their friend. I still don't work so well in a group in class. It's all, 'We've got this. We're finishing this. You do your own thing. Stay away while we do the work.' It makes me feel hurt.

My parents have helped me more than anyone to get the support I need in school and to get school to make the accommodations I need. They stay up late to do homework with me and that is not their favourite thing. When I go up to my teachers and say, 'Can I come to see you after school?' they help me. Often they don't know about my IEP (Individualised Education Program) and the help I need and I've had to advocate for myself more than once. I make sure that they know I need to be at the front of the room. I can focus more and there are less distractions. It helps me if I use highlighters and sticky notes.

Dyslexia has made me stronger and I have learned life lessons a lot earlier than most kids. I would say to anyone with dyslexia, 'We will get through this. We are survivors and we will be okay.'

Joe, 13, West Lothian, Scotland

I remember in primary when I was six or seven always being the last to finish. The teacher thought I wasn't trying and I was always trying. She made me stay in at break and finish off the work. By the time break finished I still wouldn't have finished and I'd be in even more trouble. She would say, 'Keep doing it until you're done.' By the time the others had come back from break I would still be working on the first piece and then they would be doing the second piece. I had to stay in at lunch to do the second piece and would end up taking it home to finish.

This was really hard because break and lunch were the only times I had to stop thinking about what was troubling me. This meant I didn't get that time to relax. All through primary school they kept saying I was slow and not trying. I remember I kept reversing J and P. The teacher was so negative. She kept saying I had to do my letters the right way round. They were blind to the possibility that I might have dyslexia.

Once I spent the whole day including lunch doing a piece of writing and the teacher said it wasn't good enough. She rubbed out the whole page that I had spent the whole day doing. It was soul destroying. There had been no point in me putting all that effort in. I thought, 'If I can't learn the way you are teaching me, teach the way I can learn', but I didn't say anything.

I thought I was broken; that something was wrong with me – and only me. Sometimes there would be a few who picked on me because I was slow.

I knew there were things I was good at. I would make comics – random ones featuring superheroes. I would do the drawings and my friends would do the writing for me.

In primary seven when I was 11 or 12 I had to do a leavers' presentation. I wrote things about dyslexia and how this was my experience of school. I wanted to show I wasn't ashamed of my spelling mistakes. My teacher just deleted the whole presentation.

I ended up doing a visual presentation of dyslexia. Part of this involved some of the children from the school. I sent my sister to spell cat by looking for the letters c, a and t and finding them straight away. I got my best friend to look for the same letters but he had to run around everywhere to find them as they were scattered everywhere. He represented the person with dyslexia.

By this stage I had developed a stronger character. All my struggles meant I had learnt to try my best and that was all that mattered. I may not achieve in the same way as everyone else but I could just do my best.

Then at high school I got all the help I needed. My mum went in to see them. I had already been tested for dyslexia. They realised there was no point me learning languages and put me in some specific small groups to help me with maths, English and spelling.

It was great. Such a difference. Others were going through the same things as me! We could talk about this together. I wasn't the only one struggling with it.

This has definitely made me more confident. It's great to know that I'm not alone with my struggle. The main thing for me had been that I thought there was something wrong with me and now I know there's not. I don't care what other people think about me. Confidence is the most important thing for everyone and I am happy with who I am.

Will, 13, Victoria, Australia

I wish I could meet the person who invented spelling rules – it wouldn't end nicely! I have always found English really difficult but I think it's not surprising because there isn't any sense to spelling.

I don't enjoy maths either. My mum had me diagnosed with dyslexia and I just assumed the school would take notice but everything was exactly the same. They didn't take it on board at all. They didn't give us the accommodations.

I would vomit before I went to school and my mum would cry all the way home. I thought everything's hard and I don't want to be there any more. Some of the bullies there were horrible. I was getting death threats. I had people coming up to me in the toilets saying they were going to kill my mum and dad. Someone else would stab me with pencils and scissors. The school would tell us they had dealt with it but nothing ever changed.

One teacher was the best I have ever had. Her class was under control and she took everything about dyslexia on board. She was dyslexic too. I had a fear of getting lost between the bus and school and she told me she had had the same fear. She was really supportive but she could only help me inside the school, not out in the yard.

Then my parents moved me to a tiny school, with a student number of 49. That made a large difference. There were better teachers in general.

There aren't too many options in this area, so when I had to choose a secondary school I went to the high school part of the first school I was at. I am coping a lot better. I have grown in self-confidence and the other kids are better behaved than they were.

Partly what's better is the support I have been given at school. I've had a lot of support from the English teacher who is also the year level coordinator. I also get a bit of support from other classes and I get support from my family.

It's difficult that I'm seeing my old bullies. The one who used to stab me I sit next to in Science, which is not fun. He's an idiot. The other one is much better than he was.

I have always been happy with life outside school. I have a few different ideas of what I want to do when I'm older. I would like to be a gunsmith: you design and build different firearms. I talk a lot about firearms with my dad. I would also like to go into sheep or dairy farming. I'm decently sporty and recently I have been playing Aussie rules football and cricket and I also umpire Aussie rules football. I go on long runs – 12, 14 and 16 km – I'm good with music and play the drums and a little bit of the guitar. I can read music better than I can read words. Playing the drums is a good way of releasing anger.

My dad had a terrible, terrible time at school and doesn't read, write or spell. He hates teachers and doesn't like to come to any school I've been to, besides the very small one, though he does sometimes go along with me if I really want him to. He knows a lot though. He is great to talk to.

Looking back, I was a shell of a kid. I have come a long way. You can see the growth in me.

—— #6 ——
Achieving my goals

> '**I am doing the work I am doing and dyslexia isn't going to stop me.**'

Addison, 11, Ohio, USA

What made me feel better about being dyslexic is learning. It's the teachers helping me, not having them ask why I haven't done my work; not having them think I wasn't trying when they would see me staring out into space or because I didn't finish my homework.

Homework was long. Really long. Once the nurse had to call my mom because I had a meltdown and went to her office crying with all the testing at school.

I found out I was dyslexic when I was six. Finding out helped me to understand myself. It meant I had extra teachers and that helped me too, and I had different spelling lists and that made things a bit easier. School became less of a fight. I had more time and more help, and I felt better because I didn't feel like I was stupid.

No one with dyslexia should think that they are stupid. I know your friends will study and know how to spell words and say to you, 'You don't know how to spell them.' If your friends are questioning why you don't read or spell very well, just be honest and say you have dyslexia. If you don't they will always wonder and they might make fun of you. If you're honest – not so much.

The people who have helped me most include my mom. My mom knew I wasn't a regular learner. She knew I wasn't getting it. I used to do homework with her and this year, for the first time, I didn't ask her for help. I didn't need to. My grades are decent now and I did everything on my own and I brought home 2 As, 2 Bs and 3 Cs.

I think dyslexic people are better visually and better at more hands-on stuff. I like Lego® bricks. Even when I didn't know how to read the instructions, I knew how to put complicated kits together just by looking at them.

The way I look at life, anything that happens in the world needs a machine. When I leave school I would like to do something with cars. I like the sounds cars make, how fast they go, everything about them. I like the different kinds of wheels. I like how the parts go together. I like how the engine works with oil injectors that pump in gas and then the cylinders move, which makes an explosion so your car can drive.

I am proud to be able to say that I'm dyslexic and I'm not embarrassed about it. I have had help and the people who have helped me have been kind. Everything's starting to make sense. I'm more independent. My mind is clearer.

Hannah, 18, London, England

I did well in primary school. I got good grades in my SATS. That was the trouble. As soon as I went to secondary school they expected a lot more from me than I could give. When it came to work I got very frustrated. As soon as I opened the book I would see the first question I couldn't understand and gave up on myself.

The teachers always said, 'You can do it, Hannah.' I would be in good sets. I would say, 'Please can you move me down', but because of my primary grades they thought I should continue to do well.

I begged them to move me down. I would get two questions right on a test paper and get Ds and Es and my target grades were still Bs and As. Mum contacted them because she was concerned but nothing happened. I put Catering down when we had options to choose from and they put me down for History instead.

I think the teachers thought I wasn't trying. I was one of the popular girls. Our class was the class who had fun. The teachers thought I was lazy and distracted by boyfriends and friends, but actually I couldn't do it.

If they were teaching me something I knew I would think, 'Yes, thank God.' If it was outside my comfort zone I just got overwhelmed. I couldn't take the information in and would switch off. I would get distracted and think about life, what was going on, anything really. Or I would start mucking around with the naughty kids.

I tried to get the school to let me drop History but they wouldn't. In Maths we never went over the things we had covered in class and in the next session we would have moved on to something else and I wouldn't have understood the last thing.

I do have a very clever group of friends and I tried to do what everyone else was doing to make myself feel better inside. I went to the library with them to study but would stay there for ten minutes. As soon as I got to something I didn't understand I completely shut down.

I think my mum understood. She has dyslexia and understands the barrier that makes you automatically switch off. Some other things I did reminded mum of herself. Her spelling is awful. My spelling is horrific. Spell check doesn't recognise my spelling.

In Year 11, when I was 16, Mum got them to give me a dyslexia test. This meant I had extra time on all the exams but I didn't pass one of them. I only passed the two subjects that were based on coursework.

The teachers had said to me, 'You will definitely pass.' So I always had that in my ear. I had thought I might scrape through. It was a big, big shock when I failed. Inside I knew I hadn't done enough work but so many people had said, 'You will be fine', that I started to believe it.

To be capable of anything you need the right support. Once I'd been diagnosed they put me in a special group for English for a week but it was still with my clever friends. That's why I thought I was in the same bed as everyone else.

Everyone was saying how hard the work was and how much they hated revising and how they did badly in the exams and then they all opened their envelopes on results day and got A stars. I thought, 'You fibbers.' I opened mine and everything I had hoped for was taken from me. I went home and cried with my mum. I put on the face of 'I'm the stupid one' with my friends. There wasn't much else I could do.

I had wanted to do A levels and go to university. We had all always talked about that. There must have been a part of me that thought I could do it. Or I wanted to do a course that would lead me to working with animals. I am disappointed not to be doing that.

In the end I still think it's me that's the problem – I give myself the message that I'm lazy and I don't try. The strange thing is that I'm doing an apprenticeship now, working really hard in a nursery, and at work I'm great at learning stuff. I never forget how to fill in a report or make a formula bottle. I don't know if it's because this is something I love or if it's because it's something I have been doing for a while. I think it's partly because I enjoy it. I haven't failed an exam since I left school. I had to take an ICT exam recently and I passed that. I had to take English and Maths again and I worked so hard and I passed them, which is what has made me feel better about being dyslexic. When I had to retake my Maths I was so nervous it was horrific. I had post-it notes all over my room, scribbles all over my arm. I was told if I failed I would lose my job. I passed, but if you gave me maths now I wouldn't know any of it.

I think I'm intelligent in a common-sense way but not the educational way. I sometimes wish I could have gone to uni or worked with animals but that wouldn't be me. It would be someone else.

Everyone says that I'm good at talking to people. It's always me who has to start any awkward conversations. I'm a good friend. I'm a good listener. I have to have compassion at work. But the whole failing GCSEs thing has made me lose so much confidence. It completely changed me in every way. I had been a loud, bubbly person, never shy. Now I'm much more reserved. I think I was in complete shock for a long time.

Although I feel unconfident, I feel comfortable and that I'm in my own place. I love my work and I am so lucky with my friends. They are like my own little family. Even the ones that went away to uni come back a lot of weekends. High school is a weird time. You are trying to find out who you are. I made friends in Year 7 and we are all still friends now. I wouldn't change that for anything.

Rani, 8, Madras, India

I feel better because now I am able to understand and read and write. I knew I was struggling when I was six-and-a-half and I couldn't read fluently, writing was difficult and spelling was hard.

I noticed that my friends were finding these things easier. I think some of them knew that I was finding it difficult to write. It was like I didn't know anything and I didn't have any specialisms like they did.

I go to a different school now and the teacher there helps me. I like this school as I know how to read and write comfortably, but I still like to visit my old school because I get to play with my sister there. Teachers in that school helped me too.

The most important thing for parents to do is to encourage children with their spellings. I'm good at art and math and I would like to become an art teacher when I'm older.

Sophie, 9, New York, USA

What made me feel better about being dyslexic was that I could read; that I could do it. In my last school I wasn't paying attention. Now I have moved on. I like achieving and I think reading is my speciality. Roald Dahl, I really like him. I love *Matilda*. I like *Wimpy Kid* and *Hubble Bubble*.

Some of math I find easy and some of it I find hard. I really like my teacher: she keeps us entertained. Every day is fun but just a little bit hard. Sometimes the teacher explains things or she makes us draw or play a game on the computer to explain it.

At my old school I liked my friends, but I used to be scared and anxious and worried. One girl was a bit of a bully and if anyone did something to me I would just walk away and not say anything. I joined this school in second grade and I really changed. Someone pushed me and I literally pushed them into the wall. I said not to push me. I was no longer scared every day.

When I was in kindergarten I wasn't sure if I was dyslexic. I got most of the answers right. Sometimes I would say 'drawed' and 'teached' instead of 'drew' and 'taught'. When I got into second grade I realised I wasn't changing. I couldn't get reading right. I found it hard to spell even the word 'the' and the word 'a'. I had a teacher come to my house and she had me study these words. I found them hard all the time. She said to my mom, 'You should take Sophie to see if she is dyslexic.' When the specialist said I was, my mom and dad said, 'That explains everything.'

Sophie, 9, New York, USA

Now I'm good at reading and spelling but I also like art. I want to be a fashion editor because I like drawing and making designs. I think clothes matter and I like seeing how they are designed. Some people think they are just for show but I think they fit your personality. You wouldn't wear a black top if you were all happy and sweet and you wouldn't wear a pink top if you weren't very nice. I don't know where I get my designs from. I don't know what I'm doing with my hands: they swirl around the page.

I used to think I didn't want to be dyslexic but now I'm quite happy about it. I feel everyone's different because we all have different stories and different

> I don't know what I'm doing with my hands: they swirl around the page.

personalities. I watch how people act around other people. Some don't act very nice and some do. Some of the most famous people are dyslexic. If you're dyslexic you have an amazing mind. You can see things that other people can't. You can see in 3D. I can picture walls in any colour. I can picture things how they are supposed to look.

Yasmin, 18, Surrey, England

Because I knew I was good at art I didn't try hard with my other subjects. The teachers would get angry and call my mum in but I had already switched off from a lot of school by then. The teachers spoke so fast in some of the lessons it was like they were talking in a foreign language. This flurry of words flew past me. When I could understand what they were saying, what they were teaching seemed irrelevant to my life. I would come home and say to my mum, 'What's the point of science?' She would say, 'It's in medicine, shampoo, margarine...' but I would already have lost interest.

I can imagine if someone feels not good at any subject their brain would feel so stressed and muddled at exam time. I knew I could scrape through, not because I knew the English quotes or the mathematical formulae or had memorised anything, but because I knew how to give common-sense answers to exam questions. I think I used my intuition to answer questions. Sometimes that's what they look for. You don't always have to give a direct quote; you just have to have some understanding of what the question is asking.

In Maths I didn't know my times tables. I couldn't take them in. I only know my twos, threes and tens. If I needed to answer seven times eight I would literally write seven down eight times and add them up.

I enjoyed writing in English but didn't enjoy reading or the lessons. The writing bit is creative and I didn't try to get marks with correct spellings. I thought I could get by without, though I know the marking system here is much stricter with spelling now. In a way I enjoyed maths but I didn't enjoy being taught it. I just liked answering the questions in my own way.

I couldn't have sat and revised and read the revision texts so my mum sat next to me on the sofa and read them out to me. She would notice when I had stopped listening and then go over the lines again. Sometimes we had to go over a paragraph three or four times before I could begin to take it in. Even then, by the next day, I would have forgotten some or all of it. We had two books to study for English but, if we spent some time learning about one of them, what I'd remembered about the other would disappear from my mind.

I didn't think it was a risk putting all my energy into art and the creative subjects rather than being caught up in subjects I didn't like. I had confidence I would just about get through, even though I was playing by my own rules, and I did.

Many of my friends had no idea what career path they wanted to take. For them school was harder in a way. They were under pressure to do well in everything.

When I left school I had this plan in my head to work for myself. Everyone thinks it's crazy but I would rather be in debt from starting my own company than spend three years of my life at university and end up in way more debt. I could graduate and end up working for someone who was doing what I could start doing now. I never understood why everyone was talking about uni. I didn't get the hype.

I've already got some mentoring to help me get a loan and start my own business. I'm learning all the time and it's much easier for me to learn by doing things: drawing designs, visiting factories, setting up a supply chain.

All my friends are at uni but not me. No regrets.

Freddie, 10, London, England

Finding out how many people were dyslexic and realising that I wasn't the only one who found things hard made me feel better.

Halle, 13, West Lothian, Scotland

My mum and dad wanted me to go to a different school, one that teaches children with dyslexia. I didn't want to go. It's really far away and I didn't want to make new friends and do all that again. When I went it was much smoother and easier than I expected and I had a really nice teacher. I think anyone with dyslexia should try something else if what they are doing isn't working. You have to keep trying and never give up. Keep trying to get better at reading, writing and spelling. If you give up you are never going to learn.

> I think anyone with dyslexia should try something else if what they are doing isn't working.

Also I think if I wasn't dyslexic I wouldn't be as good as I am now in maths. I sometimes do things the hard way and work things out in a much longer way. It's the first way I think of doing it and it's just to do with being me. I did a test the other day and I got 93 out of 100.

I really like history too, and learning about the Celts and the Vikings. Outside of school I like learning survival skills and I have bows and arrows. I'm into making stuff out of flint. We go up to the River Wye in Wales and there's lots of land there and the river's really nice to swim in. When I'm older I'd like to be a bush craft instructor or survivalist or naturalist, an expert in natural history.

I'm into recycling stuff and inventing things. I collect scrap metal including old cans and bicycle chains off the street and I make stuff out of them. I once made this invention: I nailed the end of the rake into the end of the broom and made a 'broom rake'. Once I got a coat hanger and made a dentist's tool and you could see right inside my mouth with it. In the garden, in one of the flower beds, I dug a pit and made an underground oven with a watering can spout stuck out of it like a chimney. I put earth on top of the stove and cooked jacket potatoes out there.

> Once I got a coat hanger and made a dentist's tool and you could see right inside my mouth with it.

I also like woodwork a lot. I made a kettle stand and a totem pole in a class at school.

On the other hand, I have found reading hard. I concentrate on the words but not actually putting them into my memory. I find it much harder to remember my spelling and my mum is so pleased when I remember to spell words like 'where' and 'wear'.

Finlay, 9, London, England

Just because you're dyslexic doesn't mean it's going to spoil your life. You can make things better by focusing on your work and asking questions. If you don't understand, ask the teacher rather than saying nothing. Sometimes I do this, sometimes I don't ask – even though I don't understand. I do know that I am really bad at some stuff and good at other stuff. Thinking like this makes me feel better.

In writing I am gradually improving. I found out I was dyslexic in Year 2 or 3. I struggled at writing English, just getting my thoughts on to paper. My reading is fine but even now I still find writing hard. On the other hand, I'm good at sport, art, design technology and maths.

I find my struggle with writing annoying but I try not to think about it. I had to move schools and leave all my friends. Since then I have been gradually improving.

In the future I know I don't want to do office work. That's boring. I want to do outdoor stuff. In this book I was reading by Roald Dahl he went to different countries for Shell in order to supply oil to vehicles. That's something I would like. Or I could be an inventor. I have thought of ideas but I haven't made lots of proper stuff. One of my ideas is a motorbike that splits in half to make a drone. The wheels split in half and they become the propellers and spread out along the side.

Hayley, 18, Glasgow, Scotland

When I was trying to decide what I wanted to work in when I left school, I kept jumping between social work and journalism. I thought I couldn't be a journalist because of my dyslexia and I knew I would have to pass Higher English. That might be a problem. The grammatical side let me down a lot at school, though I was offered extra help and extra time.

Then I realised I didn't want to do social work. I get too emotional and would want to bring all the children home with me. I started seeing writing as a way to help other people, and make people aware of issues. It would give me a big voice.

When I was 15 I talked to the English teacher about this and she started helping me.

One of my problems is that my mind goes blank when I write on paper. I know what I want to say but my hands don't know which way to move. It was embarrassing at school too because I knew no one was able to read my handwriting when I handed my work in.

I also struggled to copy from the whiteboard. Everyone else was racing ahead writing everything down and I felt it was all too fast for me. Everything was on fast forward. I had to shut my eyes to calm my mind down.

I was offered a scribe for exams. They said I would just have to say my answers out loud and the scribe would write them down but I'm a fast talker and my brain works faster than anyone else's so instead I used a computer and spell check. I was nervous for months before the exams. I was told I could take them in the library. I thought I would be the only one not in the main exam hall but, to my surprise, I went into the library and there were ten other people sitting at computers, getting the same help as me. There were also people with scribes. I realised dyslexia is not as rare as I thought. Other people had issues too.

My mum had told my primary school she thought there was something wrong and they just said I was young and had time to learn and adjust. When I was in the second year of high school my teachers thought there was something not quite right as my writing skills and my spelling weren't getting better, so they sent me to the special needs person. They had me doing 'at', 'bat' and 'cat', which was really annoying. I felt they were putting me down.

I felt so embarrassed when they diagnosed me. I thought I would be seen as stupid by everyone. I felt I had pink hair – this thing that everyone could see without me mentioning it.

I didn't like getting pulled out of class for tests with people all looking at me. It's not a nice feeling.

I remember one of my teachers in Business Studies said in front of the full class, 'Hayley I couldn't read your writing.' I almost burst into tears right there. I was so embarrassed. My parents talked to the school and then the teacher took me out of the class and apologised. She was crying. I told her I wasn't that upset, I was just worried I wouldn't get the scores I needed. After that she was the best teacher. She would give me an extension to top up my work and said I could use a computer in class.

My English teacher was the reason I got into journalism. She took so much extra time out to help me study, helping me find new ways to learn that wouldn't be upsetting for me. I owe these teachers a lot.

Eventually I told my friends. I was still embarrassed but I had started to move away from the fear that the others would think I was weird; and that I couldn't pass my exams and I couldn't do journalism.

When I opened up to the others, things began to get a lot better. Teachers helped me and my friends understood the best they could. I didn't feel on show like I once did.

I passed my exams and decided not to go to university. Instead I went to college to do a course in journalism. My goal is to run my own magazine and I feel really ambitious to achieve that.

However, if any of the other journalism students read my notes I am always embarrassed. I have to say, 'You can have a look if you want but I'm dyslexic.' My writing is not going to get any better though my shorthand is good because there is no spelling in it, only sounds.

I have already written a personal piece about my experience of dyslexia for one of the national newspapers in Scotland. Someone wrote in to the newspaper afterwards, a man called Joe. He told me I had done an amazing thing. He is dyslexic and was told he was stupid and that he wouldn't amount to anything. Now he is a businessman. The same was true of my father – he was called illiterate and there was no help for him. It still affects him now.

I think I have just started to give up being scared of dyslexia. I am doing the work I am doing and dyslexia isn't going to stop me. I'm a lot more confident now. In the past I would have rewritten and rewritten something, but now I have more confidence I will just hand it in. I won't let myself be limited. I will find a way.

7

Boosting friendship

'Together we can overcome any problems.'

Fin, 15, Buckinghamshire, England

My friends have given me confidence. They know I am dyslexic and they accept me for who I am. They know that I struggle and they don't judge. I think they like my personality, which can be very weird sometimes! They are all very confident and they have made me confident too.

This means that when someone who is younger than me, like my brother, is struggling with something I know it's all about helping each other. I know where the other person is coming from because I struggle.

One of my friends didn't find out she was dyslexic until Year 9 when she was about 13. I knew she found reading hard and she was given coloured glasses. I say to her, 'Embrace it.' It's just about talking to other people and supporting them. Together we can overcome any problems.

Fin, 15, Buckinghamshire, England

When I was seven or eight I was finding the work really hard
and I was definitely at a lower grade than everyone else. I was
taken out of class a lot to do one-to-one sessions with this

specialist who came to help, and I did activities and different sheets with her. It must have helped a bit but I didn't like doing that because I was taken away from my friends. The others would ask me why I was being taken out of class and I was definitely a bit embarrassed.

The teacher would ask a question, especially in Maths and English, and other students would be shouting the answers out and I would be picked on by the teacher and I wouldn't know the answer. Primary school was definitely not fun.

When I came in to secondary school they already knew I was dyslexic. Every morning I went to read with these people in the learning pool. This was also for disabled children and children struggling and needing help with their homework. I did that for two or three years. Then they took me off the programme. They had helped me so much they knew I was ready to work the way I wanted to.

I can definitely cope better than I used to but sometimes when the teachers ask difficult questions I won't understand. Then others in the class will come and help me.

James, 9, County Kildare, Ireland

A lot of my friends help me with words that I'm struggling with. In fact, being dyslexic has shown me how nice people are. My friends are interested in what I do. My friends say I'm better than them at things and I say it's not that I'm better, it's that we're all different. If they are struggling in their maths, I tell them, 'If you try hard enough you can do it.' It makes them feel confident. We help each other.

I'm pleased I am dyslexic and the best thing about dyslexia is that people are nice to me. Teachers are nice to me too. My teacher usually helps me if I am finding things hard.

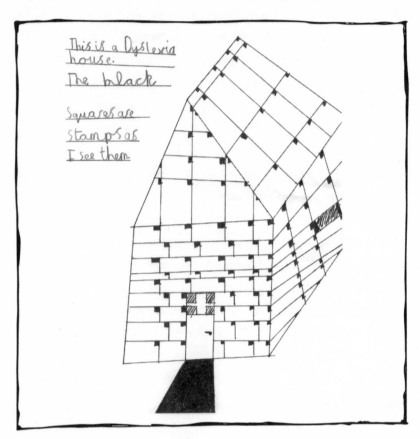

This is a Dyslexia house.
The black
Squares are
Stamps as
I see them.

James, 9, County Kildare, Ireland
'The black squares all look the same – just how I see words.'

Dyslexia is what makes me, me. At first I thought I was in a dip but I found a way to get out of it. I kept thinking I was able to do this. I kept thinking to myself, 'I can do it, I can do it.'

I'm different but in a good way. With dyslexia you don't have to think about not being good; all you have to do is try. That's not what people tell me, I tell myself that.

Since [my] first class I found reading really difficult. The words got jumbled up. At first I thought it was just because I wasn't trying hard enough. My big brother is in secondary school and he's better at schoolwork than me. My little brother is only in crèche and he finds reading easy.

I was always surprised that others found the work easier but I found a way. I used to look at the pictures in the book and think what the words would be. This worked a lot. When I went to bed my mammy would read me a book, I would look at the pictures and get the words. That's what I did to learn to read. Writing was easy; Maths is probably the easiest subject for me. It was just reading the words that was hard.

I go to a workshop now. I find it helps me with my reading. They think of nice ways to remember words. They break them up, like 'broth-er'. I feel really proud of myself when I get them right. I know if I try hard enough I can do it.

Patrick, 9, Manchester, England

I knew about my dyslexia two weeks ago when Miss mentioned it. Talking about it has helped me. I have got it off my chest by telling my friends. They were all interested and respected it. I was worried they would not understand that I struggle a bit. A couple of my friends said they knew that I was dyslexic already. I wonder if they just guessed.

We did something on dyslexia on 'Celebrating difference day'. There is something nice about it. It makes you feel different and special. What's good about being different is that no one is the same as you. Everyone else is different. Imagine how boring it would be if everyone was the same. Sometimes dyslexia does challenge you but it would be boring if things were easy all the time.

> In school we work with partners and if you get stuck with something they can help you.

English is hard because I can't really think of anything to write. Nothing pops up in my head. We were doing a story today and I couldn't think of many ideas. I forget what happens in the story. If I'm playing a game and I want to remember something I say to my parents, 'Will you remember this?' or sometimes I write a little note on my arm.

In school we work with partners and if you get stuck with something they can help you. It's good to take help from other people, just like I help my mum with the washing. Someone wanted to know how to spell 'exotic' the other day and said they couldn't find it in the dictionary, so I helped them look for it.

When I'm doing maths it helps if I think a bit and then I remember to do stuff like ask for help and use the equipment to help me. One day, near Christmas, we were doing coding. I cracked a code to make a sentence and we had to do adding, dividing, timesing and taking away. I managed to do it with a bit of help from my friends and I helped them too, so the whole table worked together.

Peyton, 10, California, USA

It is a little hard at school, especially reading, spelling and math. I am getting better. Every day in the morning I go to a special class and it helps me with my math. My special education teacher helps the most at school and my mom helps me with homework. I don't like it but I've got to do it.

These times are good for me because it's just me. The teachers are very helpful. I keep working and it kind of makes me feel better. The worst times for me are spelling tests and reading out loud. I kind of stutter and some words I don't know.

There are three of us with dyslexia and, if I don't want to hang out with my other friends, I hang out with them.

When I'm doing spelling tests I'm trying to finish faster. Sometimes I get 8 out of 12 right but I forget them all afterwards. I work hard because I want to be a vet. Animals are loving and caring to people. I can be loving and caring to them as well. They are the opposite to what people do when they are mean.

To me the best thing about being dyslexic is that it has made me a good friend. If my friends are hurt I come straight to them. Having a learning disability had made me more sympathetic to others' feelings

I know that I just have to get through school. I half like it and half don't. The half I like is that I like playing with my friends but the other half is that it is very, very hard work.

In class my mind wanders. Sometimes when I'm meant to be working I make up little stories in my head. These make me feel happier. So does gymnastics. That calms my mind down. I'm really good at the beam. It's a calm sport and it takes away some of the pressure.

Sarah, 13, Victoria, Australia

Others were finding school hard when I was, but I didn't notice. I was too busy worrying about what everyone would think. I was caught up in this fear. I heard I was dyslexic and I didn't know what it was. I hadn't heard of it before. I wondered if it was some kind of illness.

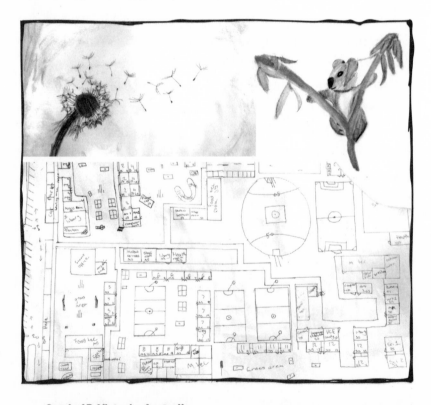

Sarah, 13, Victoria, Australia
'Dandelion', 'Koala', and 'Blueprint for a school'.

In grade five I told the vice principal about my dyslexia and I showed her what I did and what my spellings and grammar were like. Since then the school has taught the children about dyslexia and they do things in class to help dyslexic pupils. Now I'm able to talk about it easily.

The worst thing for me had been not being able to share how I felt with anyone. I thought I was the only one who had it. Then I heard two girls talking and they both were dyslexic. I went over to talk to them and I found out that eight other kids had it too. That built my confidence and I wanted us all to be treated well.

In secondary school I made this group of friends. There were about nine of us and three or four had dyslexia or other challenges. We were pretty open about them and they had a class after school to help us. We had a lot of support.

> If I am worried that I'm not going to pass a test I can talk to my friends because they are probably feeling the same thing I am.

I would say friendship is what has made me feel better. Knowing that I'm not the only one means I don't need to be afraid of it. If I am worried that I'm not going to pass a test I can talk to my friends because they are probably feeling the same thing I am.

The most helpful person has probably been my mum. She didn't know much about dyslexia because it's my dad who is dyslexic, but she has read a lot about it and she tries to help me.

I had a teacher last year who didn't understand what dyslexia was like so she didn't try to help us. That was really annoying and I felt angry about it as it made things much harder. My friends were trying to help each other because we didn't understand when we were asked questions and she didn't try to explain them.

I love soccer, swimming and I play the flute. I'm good at art. I really love art. I'm really good at soccer and play for a league, which makes me confident. I'm aiming to be a famous soccer player.

Otherwise I'd like to be an outdoor education teacher: someone who takes kids on camps and teaches them how to survive outdoors and cook for themselves. I like native animals like koalas, kangaroos and the Tasmanian devil because they make me feel I have got a friend if I feel lonely. We live in the mountain range and do a lot of hiking in the hills and play lots of games outdoors, building cubbies [playhouses] made of sticks. I'm good at designing and building things.

Georgia, 12, Buckinghamshire, England

My teacher worried that I might have dyslexia when I was in Year 2 and I went to an appointment in Year 4. I wasn't good at reading and my writing was at a lower level than all my friends. It bothered me a little bit. I thought I'd catch up and it would be fine. Now there is a bit more pressure. Sometimes my teachers forget that I'm dyslexic and that puts more pressure on me.

My friends know that I'm dyslexic. If I get something wrong, I know and they know it's not because I'm stupid, it's because I have dyslexia. I was quite happy when they told me.

I knew then that I wasn't stupid. At school I like art and I like PE – netball, swimming and gymnastics. My dad is dyslexic and he was very good at sport. He thought I might be as well.

Isla, 12, Stirlingshire, Scotland
'I love swimming because it lets me forget if something was hard at school, and have fun.'

8

Being talented

> 'What you can't do is nothing compared with what you can.'

JX, 14, Hougang, Singapore

Life has taught me that we need to discover our strengths, passions and talents so that we can work on them and excel. If you have not discovered yours yet, don't worry. Be kind and very patient with yourself in order to explore these.

We cannot let examination marks define who we are. We are much more than the numbers reflected on our report cards. We must always believe in ourselves: do our best and leave the rest.

When I was eight, my marks started to deteriorate tremendously. I couldn't understand mathematical concepts and formulae. I was always lost in lengthy and confusing maths problems. With Science, there were too many facts and difficult keywords to remember and spell out.

Qualities that I felt were part and parcel of me were abnormal to another student. I reversed my bs and ds, and ps and qs. I have problems with my short-term memory, so am unusually forgetful and unable to follow multiple but simple instructions. I frequently invent and misspell words. I kept missing deadlines too.

I was utterly frustrated and impatient with myself. I thought of myself as completely stupid, though definitely not lazy because I tried so hard. I was despondent and thought I would never be able to pass anything. A concerned relative who has a dyslexic son told my mother that I might be dyslexic and I was registered for an assessment at the Dyslexia Association of Singapore.

At 11 I was diagnosed with speech and language impairment, which, when coupled with dyslexia, felt like a double blow. My mother fought with my school for three years to get me an exemption so that I didn't have to study Higher Chinese and when this was granted I felt so relieved. I had one subject less to struggle with. A total blessing.

Dyslexia plus speech and language problems hit my self-esteem and confidence hard, especially at primary school. I was very shy and quiet as I was unable to communicate my thoughts, feelings and ideas to those around me – even my own mother. I simply could not string what I wanted to say into sentences and say them coherently. Not many listeners had the patience to wait while I processed my thoughts. Because I was depressed and not good at words, my mother sent me for art therapy. I found that I could express myself artistically. I finally discovered something that I could do pretty well.

The others in my primary class found it weird that I was fished out into another room during examinations, and that I had longer to write them, which made them envious.

Some of my classmates were also weak in Chinese but only I was exempted so they were jealous of this. I only revealed my special learning needs to a few very close classmates of mine.

I found comfort and solace in this small circle of close classmates. They helped me in my schoolwork, especially in group projects. I couldn't contribute to academic theories but when it came to art on the presentation of projects, I was both their brains and hands.

Now I am at a secondary school that specialises in art. There are many talented students in the school and we have to fight for opportunities to represent the school in competitions and for our art to be exhibited.

Art is the only subject that I can place high demands and expectations on myself; perhaps the only subject that I can excel in and get distinctions. However, educational therapists at the Dyslexia Association of Singapore have helped me with literacy, maths, examination skills, and speech and language therapy. I have learned phonics so that I can break words up, read and spell them better. I have learned to plan, organise and use mind maps. They showed me how to break down lengthy mathematical problems. I have learned how to express myself more clearly verbally and in writing. My academic work is so much better, though I still have to put in triple the amount of time and effort.

I have sessions with a counsellor called Auntie Angie and have learned to be a happier and healthier person, looking beyond my disabilities and working on my strengths and passions instead. I use mindfulness techniques taught by her whenever I am feeling overwhelmed.

JX, 14, Hougang, Singapore
'We can all shine as brightly as the stars in the Milky Way.'

Seeing people's faces light up when they see my art pieces greatly heightens my self-confidence and esteem. I have received three awards from the Ministry of Education: two Edusave Merits Awards and one Eagles Award. I was extremely proud of myself when I managed to represent my school in the Singapore Youth Festival Arts 2016 and gave a presentation on stage in school. I also clinched the 'art scholar' title after braving an interview on my own. As I have two different special needs, I hope these awards will inspire others to know they can achieve, with determination and persistence. In the future, I am aiming for an overseas scholarship and dream of being an animator for Walt Disney.

Dyslexia has given me these artistic and creative talents. My ability to think differently sometimes catches people by surprise. They question how I could have thought of some of my ideas.

Being dyslexic also makes me a more resilient, caring and understanding friend to my classmates. I think a few of them may be dyslexic and I feel lucky that I was diagnosed earlier and received help.

I think of all the people who have helped me as 'earthly angels'. I would not be what I am today without them. Mrs Lim, my ex-principal from primary school – the person whom my mother battled with to get me an exemption from Higher Chinese – has played a vital part in my life and we still meet up with her. After she left the school she still sent me PowerPoint slides and emailed me words of encouragement and support as I could no longer meet her in her office every semester to have pep talks with her.

Mrs Lim's staunch belief in me led me to start believing in myself. Many of my mother's friends, too, have boosted my morale, giving me support, showering me with kindness and tender loving care.

My mother recently told me that she thinks there is an eagle inside of me that helps me to soar above the storms of life. Maybe it is true of all of us.

Molly, 16, Stirlingshire, Scotland

As Lady Gaga would say, I'm 'born this way' and I've never really known anything different. Sometimes I wish I could spell things more easily but most of the time I wouldn't change it for the world. What you can't do is nothing compared with what you can.

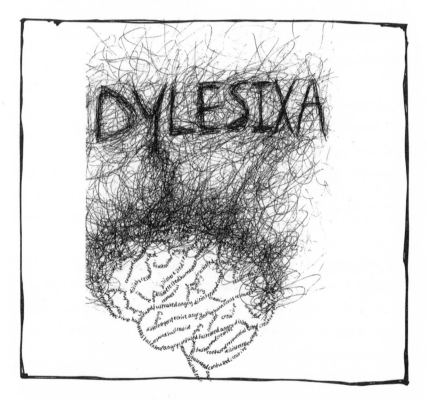

Daisy, 17, Somerset, England
'Brainstorm.'

I think when I found out it was really good to know that I just have this thing that makes my brain work differently. I come up with ideas that other people wouldn't think of.

If I have to write a story I like coming up with the ideas but find it hard to get the words down on the page – but when I'm lying on my bed thinking of random song lyrics I can do that. I'm doing a piece at the moment that is about a girl and a boy in the train station. The boy's an artist and the girl's a musician. She describes him in music; he describes her in art. They don't know each other; they just met on a dull day. Ideas like that keep popping into my head.

I want to work either in the music tech industry doing sound design, or create the sounds used on TV and radio. Or I would like to become a music therapist, either for children or adults. Maybe subconsciously I'm thinking I would like to pass on a bit of wisdom gained from my life experience. On the other hand, I have always had a love of history and I also think about being an archaeologist.

> It makes some things a bit more difficult but you can be so great at other things.

I definitely have had some insecurities. These are quite random. One is other people marking my work. This can be someone who is perfectly polite but I don't know them. Most of my teachers understand, but if you're not dyslexic it can slip your mind. It's a tad awkward.

But I don't see dyslexia as a disadvantage; it's just a different way your brain works. Sometimes it just makes you more equipped for other subjects. I have a friend who's amazing at cooking and has dyslexia. I'm great at remembering song lyrics. It makes some things a bit more difficult but you can be so great at other things.

Oliver, 8, Manchester, England

Dyslexia makes you special. It makes you different from other people.

I want to be a footballer for Manchester United. Without dyslexia I don't think I would be so good at football because I am good at knowing where to be on the pitch. Some people are greedy and never pass. If you are greedy you will never get a goal. I am able to look at the bigger picture and tell people if you don't pass the ball in time you will never score. Some people don't know that. I try to explain it and they just carry on.

If you keep the ball and someone's in front of you, that won't work. You have to pass. You have to work as a team and then when you kick a ball into the net you feel excited.

At school I find work is difficult but they help you learn. I have got stuff that helps me with my learning, like Post-it notes and a whiteboard. There are always sheets that I can learn from. I need to segment and blend: that means break the word apart then join it up together again. Sometimes I get help from the others in the class.

I'm quite good at maths but spelling is kind of difficult. My teacher helps me. I said to her the other day, 'That's the nicest thing anyone's done for me.'

Max, 17, Bay of Plenty, New Zealand

When I was much younger I didn't feel I knew anything. Everyone was so much better at school than I was and I just get left behind. I still struggle with writing things down.

I found out I had dyslexia around the second year of intermediate school when I was 12 or 13. I wasn't that surprised. It was a bit too late to find out by that time. I had already figured out my own ways to deal with some of the work but I had missed some of the staples of education that are really important to get you started.

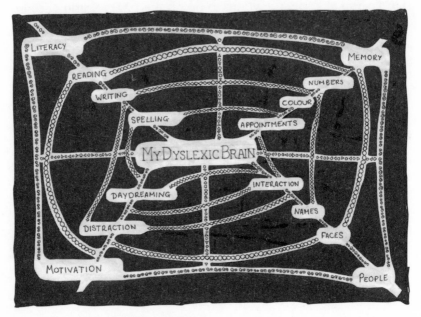

Annabel, 17, Wiltshire, England
'The words in the corners represent areas that people with dyslexia often struggle with. Along the chains towards the centre are smaller ranks within them.'

Being told I was dyslexic gave me an explanation as to why I was so terrible at schoolwork no matter how hard I tried. It was reassuring and gave me something to say when people said to me, 'Why is your handwriting so bad?' Being able to say 'I'm dyslexic' was like a little shield, even if they then go on asking questions.

The best thing about dyslexia happened when it came to doing any spatial thing at school in crafts or art. You just excel more than anyone else and you go, 'This is where I sit.' They are winning at maths but when it comes to this sort of stuff you're right at the top of the pack. Everyone should just find out what they're good at. Everyone is good at something. Everyone needs to hear that.

I'm very good at 3D, the hands-on stuff, and I'm quite good at Science and the geometry side of Maths. Because of this I have already started working part time as a mechanical engineer for a company that makes packaging for kiwi fruit. I enjoy it heaps. It just clicks with me. Shapes and 3D things are right there and you can touch them.

> Everyone is good at something. Everyone needs to hear that.

When I'm not working I'm finishing my education. When I was younger our family went travelling for a year in a caravan all over New Zealand and for that year we were all home-schooled. That was something else that clicked with me. I found I could go at my own pace, find my own way round things. So I left school and Mum started teaching me. Now I do correspondence courses. I send my work off and they mark it.

Molly, 13, Buckinghamshire, England

Dyslexia is definitely a different way of being creative. I like drawing and putting ideas on to paper. From when I was little, in nursery, my drawing book was really full, packed with lots of stuff, and my brother's was empty.

I want to become a textiles designer. I love clothes and the way you can express yourself, and there are so many different styles. I always thought of art and design as a hobby, but other people said I was really good at art and I started to say I wanted to work in the arts.

My great aunt helped children with dyslexia and she recognised it in me very early on. I was definitely in the group at the bottom of the class but, because I went to an academic primary school, everyone was a bit smart.

Molly, 13, Buckinghamshire, England
'Molly daydreaming about making clothes.'

I much prefer the school I go to now because it is creative and a specialist art college. I really enjoy art and textiles at school. My family is quite creative and whenever I went to my aunt's house we used to make things.

At school now I love the subjects that I love and have improved a lot on the other subjects. I went from a reading age of 9 to a reading age of 12. Every day I went into a reading group and read to someone. There were times I got angry if I couldn't remember a word but it was fine because it took me a little longer and then I got it.

At school at the moment I like Art, Textiles, Wood Tech and Science. In Music when my friends hear a garage band they think it sounds good, but I think it should be different. I am used to thinking a different way. I solve maths problems in a different way. I visualise them.

Beatrice, 9, London, England

Sometimes I think, 'I'm dyslexic. Yay!' I'm good at making up stories and drawing pictures and I have a great vocabulary – but I can't spell and I find writing and reading difficult. I think my vocabulary is good because I have seen a lot of movies and they say a lot of long words in those. I used a great word today – 'quivered' – and I spelt it right.

We tested me for dyslexia about two years ago. I felt relieved to find out and I feel as if I have different abilities to everybody than just being normal and the same. I'm very creative. I can make a stick and a few leaves into a pretty flower. All I need is that and, if I want to make it pretty, I use different coloured leaves. I see things and think, 'That could be of some use', and then I sit and make something with it.

I have very bad spelling. It's annoying if teachers say, 'The point is made but can't you spell it correctly?' For example,

I spell melon 'meleon'. Sometimes the teacher says, 'It doesn't matter about the spelling,' and I say, 'Yay!'

Elijah, 12, London, England

When we get to do art in school it's easy for me. It's not, 'How did you get that wrong?' No one is telling me that. I am good at drawing facial expressions. I have done that from a young age. I like showing the reflections. I like the shines.

Elijah, 12, London, England

When I read books I get this aching in my belly. They bore me. My eyes are moving around the page too much and I feel stressed. It's all too plain and it's got no movement. You need to read a few chapters to get into the story. That's why when I leave school I would like to draw comics. With comic books you just need to look at the pictures. It's so much easier.

Sometimes I get distracted. The teachers say, 'Do the work', and I am confused about what I am meant to be doing. I realised when I was younger that I didn't have the same ability as the others. In Maths they were really quick at sums that took me ages.

I still struggle with reading. When I spell something wrong and my friend is looking at me because to them it's an easy word, it's hard to say, 'I'm dyslexic.' They could say I was lying. Some people say, 'Yes, sure.' In any case you can't just go on saying that forever.

Daisy, 14, West Sussex, England

I can see my dyslexia coming through my art and through my creative work. In doing that I get away from academic stuff and it makes me feel a lot freer. If I wasn't creative I think being bad academically would destroy me, but having the art and the drama brings me back up.

> I like the freedom and the independence that comes with creativity.

It was a relief to know I was dyslexic – it means I'm not just weird. I wouldn't be as happy without it. I would feel trapped. I like the freedom and the independence that comes with creativity. It's who I am and I don't think I'd be me without it.

I didn't start reading until Year 2 when I was about seven. Before then I loved being read to but I didn't want to read. I would read a page and then read the same sentence on the next page and I would get it wrong. It was very frustrating. Maths is the worst lesson ever. I just don't like numbers. I don't like the way they work. I feel overcrowded with numbers in my maths book. They are piling up and up, and I don't know what to do with them.

Daisy, 14, West Sussex, England
'Mirror image of the word "dyslexia".'

Even though I'm bad at spelling I make money writing short children's stories for four- to eight-year-olds. I have a little sister and advertise this to the mums in her class. I find out what the children like or a challenge they are trying to overcome and use aspects of that in the stories. I type them on to parchment paper, because I can't stand writing, and tie them up with ribbon. For one of the girls I wrote a story about a necklace and tied a necklace around the story. For a boy I did the same but with a soft toy.

If I see a jumble of letters when I am trying to get a word out, I have to form things in my mind before I can see what the word is. An 'S' is hands – people to help me. An 'L' is a pencil snapping – frustration. 'I' is a pause button because I feel I should have a pause button and everything will slow down.

I have always wanted to be an actress since I was three or four when I performed little plays to my family. I can get into the mind of a character. I can leave my own mind – I don't need it any more – and change my own voice for a character's voice.

I did the school play this year and it was a lot more lines than I have learned before. I was getting panicky and the teacher was getting angry with people who hadn't learned their lines. At one point she threw her script on the floor and stormed out of the room. Luckily that wasn't on my bit.

I make lines stick by going through them, with Mum or someone else reading a line. I get someone to test me and then test me again. I have tried recording them but it didn't work. I listened a few times but I was just picking up on my own voice and feeling self-critical.

Fiona, 9, County Kildare, Ireland

Recently, while I was visiting my mam's family in Cork, I saw a blanket my great aunt was knitting. She showed me how to hold needles and wool, and gave me a book on knitting. My granny gave me a present of a home-made blanket. Now I feel like knitting is in my blood.

I am so proud at how good my knitting is. I'm knitting a scarf for my teacher and my resource teacher. I'm knitting squares and I'm going to stitch them together into a blanket. It's a mix of rainbow colours. I might give it to my dog, Toby. It feels kind of good when I've finished something and it is fun and relaxing.

I found out I was dyslexic last year. I didn't like the dyslexia test. I got some spellings wrong and read some words wrong. Being good at other things makes me feel better.

I had two bad falls in horse-riding last year and gave up but now I want to try again. My mum says I am excellent at making a determined effort to do things, and that makes me proud.

Joe W, 15, Bedfordshire, England

The way I look at problems is different from the way that other people look at them. I'm extra confident with the things I'm good at but when I'm talking about a subject I'm not good at, I lose confidence a bit.

I like being good at Maths and I'm also good at Design Technology and enjoy them both.

I have always been bad at English. With Science and Maths you have an answer that is logical. With something that is not logical you can write anything and get marks and I don't understand how to do that.

I am good at Computer Science and spatial reasoning. I want to go into automotive engineering, anything to do with cars, or 3D designing.

In Design Technology we had to design lights. Mine was a desk light but I ended up designing mine and three other people's as well. I find it easy to visualise something like that in my head before I write it down. I prefer to do it in that order.

Charlie, 17, London, England

If I was running a school I would provide a space so that people with some form of dyslexia could go there and be tested and they could find better ways to help you. Maybe if I had been younger when they spotted it there would have been more to help me. I think it's difficult to help me at the age I'm at.

I was always labelled 'not good at maths' when this shouldn't have been the case. Schools put you in boxes and leave you there.

School said to me when I was 11 that they thought I had something but couldn't say it was dyslexia. Now I am told that I have problem-solved my way through school.

> I was always in lower sets for Maths and suddenly became good at it in Year 10, when I was 15. It popped out of nowhere.

I was always in lower sets for Maths and suddenly became good at it in Year 10, when I was 15. It popped out of nowhere. I suddenly started getting As. I'm now doing A level Maths. It's quite tough but I feel like I am coping. I'm also doing Art and Economics. The teachers say I approach maths problems differently. I was recently doing integration and I came up with the answers really easily. When it got to the harder ones my formula didn't work so I was screwed for the last bit.

Art is one of my stronger subjects. This has been true since I was young. I have always been drawing. I'm not entirely sure what I want to do, but the fact I can do maths and art might lead me to architecture. A lot of people can't do both. The mind has two sides, creative and logical, and I feel I have both. Someone told me recently that architects are often dyslexic and that makes sense because they are meant to be spatially aware.

Alexander, 11, London, England
'There are two sides to me and everyone with dyslexia – one with pictures, one with words.'

YOUR MIND   MY DYSLEXIC MIND

DYSLEXIA

BUT DYSLEXIA HAS HELPED ME...

Think Spatially

Problem-solve

18 27 36 45 54 63

see patterns and similarities
in things others may not

Charlie, 17, London, England

'Your mind' and 'My dyslexic mind'.

Emma, 9, Renfrewshire, Scotland

As soon as I'm on a tennis court and get in gear I have fun, I forget I'm dyslexic and I don't have a care in the world. I want to be a famous tennis player when I'm older. A lot of people have dyslexia and some people who don't have dyslexia can't do the stuff you might be able to do.

Playing tennis is what makes me feel better. I think being dyslexic helps me know where to be on the court, where to be before the ball bounces. Coaches have said I'm very good at listening and I pick things up quickly. The coach used to give notes but now he does videos rather than writing down the shot he wants me to do. I love that I get to play against my friends. I like that you don't know what shots are going to happen and you might learn from one of the shots that they do.

Callum, 9, Renfrewshire, Scotland

There are a lot of things I'm good at, including Minecraft, Lego® and climbing. I love how fast I pick them up. I only started climbing last year. There are five levels and I'm already at level four. I like how they move the holes to make climbing more complicated. It's like solving a puzzle. Sometimes they say, 'You can only use the grey holes' or, 'You can only use the blue holes' to make it harder.

With Minecraft I like how you can build anything you like. I would like to be an architect, I would like to build a radio station and on the outside the building would look like a radio. The speakers would be the windows.

If I'm daydreaming in class, sometimes my mind goes into things that have happened in the past, but sometimes I think about what I can design in the future.

When I found out I was dyslexic it answered a lot of questions for me. Part of me was delighted. I thought this helped me to understand myself.

Keri, 15, North Ayrshire, Scotland
'Piecing together the jigsaw.'

Some of my friends noticed I was finding the work hard. One friend sits near me and said, 'Do you want me to help you?' and she sometimes does. Someone at my table was mean to me because of the number of reading points I had and said, 'Don't you know how to read?' I was crying on the inside but not on the outside when he said that, something I have learned to do.

Jarred, 14, Aruba, The Caribbean

Thanks to being dyslexic I learned to draw fast and I got a lot better in a very short time. I only started drawing last year, and before this I didn't even know I might be good at it. I taught myself by watching YouTube and learning new techniques. I now have more than 1300 people following me on Instagram to see what I will draw next. I think this is one reason why I've never been ashamed about being dyslexic.

From my first year of school I had trouble writing and learning to read. My parents suspected that I was dyslexic quite quickly as my dad, grandfather, uncle and two cousins all have dyslexia. I know I made a lot of spelling mistakes and needed more time to study than other kids. It took me way more effort than it took my sisters. My mom and dad struggled so hard for me, fought with teachers and nobody would help them. They told me that every place they looked for help they got a closed door. On Aruba there's no help so you are on your own, and because of this Mom learned how to help me.

When I was getting bad grades the school told me I had to go to a special school for not so smart kids. My parents fought back harder and took my IQ test to the school proving that I was smart, even though my grades at the time showed otherwise. Sometimes I would learn for hours and days, only to get a bad grade, but my parents never pushed me to achieve more and more. They never made it a problem if my marks weren't high. They knew I was always giving my best.

Now I am doing well. Because the school didn't give me help I have had to adjust to the school system as it is. I am managing and doing great all by myself, learning by myself and getting good grades.

My mom has been chronically ill for years and I will always ask her if she is okay, if she's feeling tired and if she is okay to drive. I always carry groceries or laundry or anything heavy for her. I play with my nephew, even though he is much younger, because I know it makes him happy.

At school if I write something on the board and it's wrong, I just say, 'I can't help it, I have dyslexia.' My family has always told me that this is nothing to do with me being smart or being dumb. I don't know what I will end up studying but my parents say they have no doubt I can go to college and be successful. It is great that they are backing me in the way they do. I still can't tell the time on an ordinary clock or remember all the months in the year in the correct order, but I am happy and doing well. Life is looking up.

9

Being diagnosed

> 'I thought if I was dyslexic and I could still do well it would make me happy and make me proud of myself.'

Eddie, 14, Manchester, England

With me, the dyslexia diagnosis was what really helped. After I found out, when I was ten, I was happy because I knew my teachers would do something to help me.

Before this they would just leave me to do work by myself, which felt like I was being punished for not keeping up to everyone else's standards. This meant I was expected to improve my grades when they weren't helping me at all. They kept making me do my work again and again. I would know what to say in my head but couldn't put it down on paper.

I thought when I was diagnosed that my friends would tease me about it, but, because they can see it for themselves, they don't tease me. The diagnosis means I get to use a laptop and have extra time.

My mum had no support when she was at school. Her friends took the mick out of her and said she was dumb. The school thought she was dumb. This must have been tough for her. She was the only one in her family who didn't get into a grammar school. She says it helps her knowing now because she can work out strategies to help her in her work. She has to read things out to herself a couple of times, even if it's just an email to one of her colleagues.

At secondary school at first I had a teaching assistant with me as I got used to the school. Eventually I didn't need her because the teacher was helping me and things were easier.

Some people can't understand my writing – I can just about read it myself. Spelling and reading is what I find hard. I'm top set in Maths but when it comes to tests I struggle to remember.

My dad is teaching me to remember patterns and drawings by using mind maps and pictures. For an ellipsis he draws a cliff as a sign of keeping something hanging on. Visually is how I prefer to learn.

In Geography in one of my tests I got the equivalent to an A. I think that's because it's all visual. It's simple: you see it and describe it and put it into writing. At the moment we are doing coastal erosion. You can see that.

School gives me three lessons a week, one-to-one. I have coloured books and coloured overlays. Some people are afraid to ask for some of these things because they are very different from what everyone else is using, but as long as it's helping me, I'm not bothered.

Henrie, 13, Manchester, England

When I was younger I was really stubborn and never wanted to work. When we were given longer words to learn I would get angry if I didn't know the word. This made me so mad I would disrupt the classes and not listen to the teacher and not care. That the other kids could do it and I couldn't – that made me mad too.

Isaac, 10, Lothian, Scotland

Then I was told I was dyslexic. I hadn't heard of this before. At first I went a bit mad again. I was stroppy for a couple of days and then it didn't bother me. When I was angry it was because I was struggling. Then I realised I would stop getting angry if I stopped struggling. I realised I had to work at my lessons. It made me work a bit harder. I thought if I was dyslexic and I could still do well it would make me happy and make me proud of myself.

I started working very hard. It made my mum and dad a lot happier with me. They always used to be disappointed with me because of my behaviour. When my teachers used to phone I could hear from my parents' voices that they were upset.

I went from being really bad to really good. My school helped me and that helped a lot. Instead of getting mad I would try to work and if I couldn't understand I would ask the teacher.

> I started getting on well with my teachers. It's hard to be bad for a teacher if you really like them.

In the first year of secondary school I was in set one for English. I started to get big headed and started messing about in class. I thought I was the best. Then I got moved down and I started working harder again. People in set one used to distract me so I'm happy to stay in the set I'm in.

I started getting on well with my teachers. It's hard to be bad for a teacher if you really like them. I saw that they would understand. They wouldn't get mad at me for not knowing something. They are good at understanding other people.

A lot of famous people have dyslexia. They are good examples for kids with dyslexia. I think they did what I did. They used dyslexia as a reason to work harder and improve and get better. It's not a bad thing when you realise that and you can overcome it and start to feel more confident. Then you can forget about it and focus on other things. It's a good reason to do your best.

When you are dyslexic you can see people doing good and see people doing bad. We have experienced both sides. When you start doing well and if you are happy with yourself, you will have a better future.

There was one time my mate tried to have a fight with my other mate. The other one was trying to say sorry but the first one was still wanting to fight. I tried to calm it down. I'm good at seeing both sides and understanding; not being selfish or biased.

When I am older I would definitely like to be in sport. I am good at football. I like boxing and athletics, a lot of sports. Because I can understand both sides it helps me understand what other people on the sports pitch are thinking. I try to work out what the other team are bad at. I try to take advantage of weaknesses in the opponent.

Ramu, 9, Madras, India

When I was seven years old I was finding reading, writing, math and spellings difficult. It was all confusing for me. The other children were finding things easier and it felt like I didn't know anything and I didn't have any speciality like they did.

I was scared about performing in exams and I thought I'd never succeed in my life.

The best thing that my teachers did is to help me and explain things in a way that I can understand. I found out I was dyslexic and then I got to do what I am good at. Also I got help in places where I had problems like reading and writing. I want to be a scientist and I am good at art and design.

Now I can read and write better and do the things the other kids can do. I am enjoying school and looking forward to going to a new one.

Parents can always encourage their children by saying, 'You can do it!'

Kane, 15, Merthyr Tydfil, Wales

I left primary school at 11 with a reading age of zero. At primary they would take me out of class and tell me to read a book with a woman but it wouldn't help. I would recognise certain words but at other times I would see the words backwards and I wouldn't know what to do. Trying to learn to read was this blur. I didn't understand what was going on.

A lot of the time I just wondered what I was doing wrong. All my friends were excelling and I would think, 'Why can't I do this?' It was really sad.

Only my friends knew I was struggling. Now my mum knows how I feel but then I just thought I'm not that intelligent.

Dyslexia got picked up straight away in high school and my reading age started going up. I don't see why no one in primary noticed. It was a big relief when I found out and my grades started to improve. It had been so difficult with all my friends on a higher tier when I was on the lower tier.

Now my confidence is so much improved. I'm willing to speak about anything I find hard to my dyslexia teacher and she has helped me the most. If anything is on my mind I can tell her. She said she could tell I was dyslexic very quickly because I was so articulate and my reading and written work didn't match that.

One of my hobbies is MMA (Mixed Martial Arts), and when I leave school I want to go to university and train to be a PE teacher or MMA coach. One of the reasons I think I would be a good teacher is because of the experiences I have had. They have made me more focused to help people who are struggling. What happened to me has made me more compassionate and it's given me extra skills that help me understand others. I'd advise any child who is struggling to try to mention it. See if you can get tested if you can.

School is easier for me now. The only time I've had someone saying anything about my spelling is when I'm in a class with high set people. One of them said, 'Why can't you spell that?' I'd missed two letters or put them the wrong way round.

One problem I do have is when teachers don't write on the board but read something out to the class. When it's bigger words or a sentence it's harder for me to write. Then I ask someone next to me, 'How do you spell it?' and the teacher will shout at me for talking.

My SpLD [Specific Learning Difficulties] teacher has given me a laminated pass for me to show supply teachers who don't know me so they will write things down for me or give me a hand-out. Most of my teachers know to give me hand-outs. Teachers who don't know me are one of the main problems.

Roísín, 18, County Carlow, Ireland

My big brother is really intelligent and he was reading Harry Potter when he was little. I was struggling with little Ladybird books. Finding out I was dyslexic made me realise that my reading problems weren't my fault. I thought this was brilliant. I screamed it from the rooftops. I never thought I would achieve in my life what I have now, but for that one day, I was very proud.

My mother had spotted something wasn't right and she had me tested. From that day, when I was six, I definitely became easier on myself.

> Numbers are my strength. I can see problems in a 3D way. It's like looking at a road map that makes perfect sense.

I remember in those early years hating reading in class and hoping the teacher wouldn't pick on me. The words would jump around. What I saw was different from everyone else. The 'big dog' would become the 'dog big'. I decided I had to find a way to hide this – I told the teacher I didn't want to read out loud and he didn't ask me. Once I found out I was dyslexic, people said, 'Ah that's why she's reading like that.'

I gained a new confidence and 12 years on I am studying for my leaving certificate. My subjects are Irish, English, Maths, French, Geography, Chemistry and Accounting.

I think dyslexia has made maths easier for me. Numbers are my strength. I can see problems in a 3D way. It's like looking at a road map that makes perfect sense. On top of this, my imagination is completely random, which is great for English. We did an essay about what we might find in a time capsule. I put Schrödinger's cat in the box without opening the box and knowing whether it was dead or alive. My teacher thought it was brilliant!

I'm going to study primary school teaching at university. I want to become a primary school teacher and would like to help people when they're little to figure out all the big stuff like reading and writing. I want to make it fun and easier for them. I think if I teach in a different way, instead of the usual mainstream way, I might be able to pick up on someone with dyslexia in my classes more quickly.

When I found out I was dyslexic I knew I wasn't just a bit slower. I found out that my mind works completely different to everyone else's. I'm not as quick but still as smart. Not dumb. I'd say to anyone with dyslexia to embrace it and find out the way you learn best. If you're a visual learner go with that; if you learn through writing go with that. Go with your strengths and don't try to follow anyone else.

Reggie, 9, Buckinghamshire, England

I felt a bit relieved when I found out I was dyslexic because I was hoping I wasn't just thick. Before this I thought I was just not that smart. Also I'm pleased I didn't go through all those tests for nothing and I think I've become a little bit more confident. I think the school might understand me more now, but I still find things difficult.

I think the dyslexia tests were in Year 3 when I was seven or eight. I was struggling in Literacy and Maths. Then school gave me a little bit more help in Year 4 and I went to a dyslexia tutor and did some reading and spelling.

Mum told me life's not all about doing well at school. She said that lots of dyslexic people are talented and I like that fact. I think if I wasn't dyslexic I would be more worried about how I was doing. I work hard at literacy and maths and I still do as much as I can in pottery and art. I like making things in 3D. I am trying to do my best so I do well in my life. The one thing I'm trying not to be is a plumber because I don't want to be scooping out poo.

> Mum told me life's not all about doing well at school. She said that lots of dyslexic people are talented and I like that fact.

Iliana, 10, London, England

When I was finding things hard and everyone else knew what they were doing, it didn't feel good. I felt like they knew about things and I didn't. Now it feels...not easier...but that it makes sense. The diagnosis answered a question for me.

Before I found out, the way they taught me was hard for me to understand. When I am taught in a different way I can understand things better. I have been taught tricks to help me learn. I play lots of sport like running and football, and they make me feel better too.

Adam, 10, County Kildare, Ireland

When I was told I was dyslexic everything clicked. It explains who I am and I felt relieved that I know about it and what it means for me.

Adam, 10, County Kildare, Ireland

I found it hard at the start of school, not knowing why I was different. I would come home crying and frustrated. Spellings never clicked with me. I couldn't concentrate. My school told me I couldn't be diagnosed until I was eight.

When I was tested I think I hadn't realised how hard I had found things previously. A lot changed after this. I was given easier spellings and easier books to read. I go to a dyslexia group and we do Maths and English there. As a result of this, my spelling and reading have definitely got better.

I like so much stuff. I do MMA (Mixed Martial Arts), football, sculling, Gaelic and chess. I am also good at acting. It's hard to choose what I want to do when I'm older because there are so many things I like.

Sam, 16, London, England

I seem to be good at problem-solving. I come at things from a different angle. I usually go round a problem and come back to the same answer as other people. This kind of creative, different thinking really does help. It gives me a slight difference, almost an edge. No one else would think of some of the things that occur to me.

I think I knew I was dyslexic from primary school. I have a memory of doing a piece of work. Everyone did it the same way besides me and I did something completely different. I think it was a puzzle. Everyone was making it into a square shape and I created something to pull things along. I remember the teacher commenting on that.

The school picked up dyslexia because of my reading. It was quite bad and I needed special support. I remember not wanting to read out loud in class. I never had my hand up and the teacher would pick on me. I was terrible. I was thinking, 'I know I can't do this. I really can't read this.' I seem to remember reading ahead and skipping lines. Everyone else would get very confused. There were always words I couldn't pronounce.

There was support in secondary school but I didn't want it so much then. I understood dyslexia better and I accepted it and was no longer concerned. When I was younger I didn't realise what was going on. I thought, 'I'm bad at English, I'm bad at spelling and I'm good at Maths. I'm bad at one thing and good at another.' The early intervention had helped me to accept myself for who I was. I starting thinking, 'It's not too bad really.' In primary I had thought, 'Why can't I read? Why aren't I as good as other people?' By secondary school I thought, 'Oh well.'

Now I'm doing A levels in Biology, Psychology and History. My essay writing is a lot better. In Year 7 it was difficult to write a lot of words, but I think the teachers have helped me a lot with essay writing.

In GCSEs I must have concentrated so hard on English I did better in that than in Maths, which was my best subject. I was amazed. I had started writing much better. A story I had written for one of my mocks was so much better than anything I had done before. My English marks started going up from there. My English teacher was really good at getting me to write well, with detail and structure. She gave me some one-on-one time when I was struggling.

When I look back I see dyslexia as a positive thing. I answer questions a bit differently, but I still get the marks.

Rory, 13, Stirlingshire, Scotland

When I was five a teacher told my mum I had problems and Mum found out I had dyslexia.

You don't know you are vulnerable then and there are not the same expectations of you. I didn't really mind about it in the early days. I kind of realised when I was seven and it didn't bother me, but when I was older it was a bit of a problem. When you are older there is more embarrassment.

Ryan, 13, Victoria, Australia

It's very important to get an early diagnosis and not to let it scare you. I think my mum has always known I was dyslexic. To start with I was probably in the same group at school as everyone else, but when the years got higher I started realising I was staying at the same level while everyone else was moving up.

If you have really nice friends, who don't just pretend to be your friends, tell them. If someone comes up and wants to know about it, we get into a conversation. They can help you if you are having trouble. On my table they don't give me the answer to a maths question but they give me pointers.

I have found maths hard, definitely, and I had trouble with spelling and reading. Reading is okay for me now and spelling has improved. Tutors have helped me as they teach one-on-one. This means it's more focused on you. In a class people are going to be at different levels.

I like sports and I like using my imagination and I like reading books, a combination of things. I used to want to be a singer, then an actor, then in the army, then a basketball player. Now I don't really know but I have a lot of ideas. I like having debates. I have been told that when you get older there's a debating society that you can get into at school. I'm looking forward to that.

#10
Working harder

> 'Determination keeps me learning. I never
> give up. I always keep trying.'

Patrick, 17, Canterbury, New Zealand

I was really sad as a young kid. I wanted to be good at school
and I just wasn't. I always found things harder: maths, reading,
English... I thought everyone was the same until I was eight
when I realised things were different for me.

I think the other kids noticed it because I was really
flustered and stressed. I used to push on my eyes with my
palms, I thought that would make the stress stop, but it didn't
cure anything.

When I was at my most stressed I thought I wouldn't ever
be able to do better. I would be freaking out like this and
one teacher would say, 'Patrick, you're putting up walls.' She
was trying to get me to have a positive mindset but I was
a 12-year-old boy who couldn't read and so it wasn't very
productive. I get what she was trying to do, but it wasn't what
I needed.

At other times I thought I could do better, because I did want to. I knew there were other people with dyslexia there, other people like me, and that did help.

One other thing that helped was that my parents put systems in place to help. Mum realised that she was sending me off to school with my mind completely jumbled up after giving me too many instructions.

Instead, she structured my morning so I knew I had six things to do. She didn't change this as it would mean I would forget something as my chain of thought would have been interrupted. The six things were:

1.   Make your bed.
2.   Open your curtains.
3.   Get dressed.
4.   Have breakfast.
5.   Get your bag.
6.   Put your lunch in your bag.

These things seem basic but they meant I knew what I was doing and they didn't confuse me.

Some days at school it was so challenging to complete one task, but Mum's system meant I knew I had started the day with six already done. She says now she knew she needed to help me help myself or I wouldn't have been able to manoeuvre myself into day-to-day life as an adult when I was older.

I also remember in Year 9 I did a creative writing story and it was really good. I was given a grade for it and I also was given the grade that I would have got if my spelling had been correct. It was a really good experience and a really horrible experience at the same time. I had written this cool and amazing story but still this thing I couldn't control had let me down. So that sucked. When it happened I was annoyed, but now I realise that the message I was being given was pretty awesome. The teacher did that for me. If I'd just been given the lower mark that would have been more disappointing.

Instead of doing a foreign language I did extra English when I was 13 or 14, and this means that now I am able to be in the mainstream English class, which is pretty awesome.

By the time I got to Year 11 when I was 15, I was getting really good marks and they tried to take away my reader and writer and my extra time. We had to fight with the Education Board who were saying I wasn't dyslexic any more. In fact I have dyslexia, dyscalculia, dyspraxia and Irlens syndrome, which is a problem with the brain's ability to process visual information.

When it all gets too much, my strategy is to have what I call a 'power cry'. I cry for ten minutes and then I carry on working. It's not socially acceptable to say that in New Zealand but...whatever. You can't beat a good cry. You feel so great afterwards.

What was great was that we found out when I was a bit older that I was good vocally and good at drama. I'm already working as an actor. I do a lot of stage work and have recently been busy doing a lot of auditions. In New Zealand unless you make your own work, you don't work and I love creating theatre. I really want to go to the top New Zealand drama school, Toi Whakaari.

I'm in my final year of high school now and studying Drama, English, Music, Media Studies and RE [Religious Education]. I'm pretty excited about leaving but I'm also loving the classes I'm taking. English is challenging me and it's good to be challenged: reading books and analysing them. They said I would never be able to do this. It is hard work definitely – and there's this real stigma about being dyslexic that means you have to be at the top bit of the class.

There are great relationships between me, my parents and the school. They have all put so much effort into me. Without them I couldn't be in an exam room for three hours. They had to put things in place to make sure I can do that.

> When it all gets too much, my strategy is to have what I call a 'power cry'.

Kids with dyslexia deserve the best. School is going to be really hard for us. We deserve just as much as everyone else. We just need to try harder; we need to take different routes to get where other people get to. We are not stupid people. We are intelligent. People need to know that and we need to make sure they do.

Luke, 10, Manchester, England

The best thing for me about dyslexia is that I have to try harder. People who think they are good at things might choose the easiest route, but even the easiest thing is quite difficult for me. Determination keeps me learning. I never give up. I always keep trying.

My spelling and my reading were tough. I used to read really thin books back in Year 5. Now I'm in Year 6 I read really thick books, so hard work really helps. Overlays help me with my reading. I use coloured see-through card, buffed paper and word searches. I feel proud of myself at how much I have progressed.

My friends help me with my spellings. They try to find a word with the same sound in it. Say I wanted to spell 'should', one of my friends on my table would try to find the word 'would', and because they sound the same I can just change the 'sh' to a 'w'. In Literacy, sometimes people don't want to read, but I ask to read and my partner helps me. Last week I was reading a text about Usain Bolt.

My mum and my step-mum help me too. They help me with spelling, reading and homework and my sister helps with my spelling, even though she's younger. Books help me because, when I read them, if I have been spelling a word wrong and want to know how to spell it, I can look in a book or a dictionary and try to find the word.

I have found Maths quite hard but I'm getting better at it. I felt I couldn't do it but I kept trying. The worst thing a teacher can do is just tell you the answer. I would say, 'Don't just tell me. Help me get it right; help me get better.'

I think dyslexia is good because no one is normal and no one is the same. Everyone's different. I'm good at building things and making stuff with Lego® like spaceships and boats. I'm good at other things too. When I was on holiday last year I swam 100 m, some of it underwater. I was looking for things under the water like the people who go scuba diving. I would like to be a marine biologist when I'm older because I'd get to study fossils and find out what they are.

Ryan, 11, London, England

When I was eight I struggled at English and wasn't doing well at spellings. I was put in a group where I would find it easier to learn. I did find it easier there but I still found work hard.

It was confusing at school. Other people could do the work. I thought they must be working better than me so I tried to do it better but it didn't go too well. Then when I was told I was dyslexic we progressed on my English and it really helped me. It was mainly comprehension that I worked on. I wasn't writing enough information or detail. Now I'm proud of the results in my last tests, 78 per cent and 88 per cent in comprehension. This has made me feel better. Whenever I do badly at stuff I know I will always struggle but I can progress.

> I know I can improve myself and, if I succeed, I feel much better.

In life I would say my strongest subject is Science. I wouldn't say I'm the best but it's one of my best things, and Maths too. I like the fact that I can learn stuff I have never learned before such as particles and materials and states. I might want to be a scientist when I grow up but I'm not sure as I haven't planned my future.

The one thing that made me feel better about having dyslexia is that I know I can improve myself and, if I succeed,

I feel much better. It's hard to feel that you are struggling but good to feel that you can improve. It's really hard to get to the top but you know you will get there eventually. It's really helped having extra lessons. I know that I'm different but that's okay.

Douglas, 9, London, England

Every time I tried to read it got trickier and trickier and trickier. One day I knew the word, the next day I didn't know it. I was quite frustrated. When I was told I had dyslexia I was pleased that I knew why this was. Now I study this book *Toe by Toe* with Billy who is a support teacher at school, and working through this book helps me read and write more easily. I also read with him in the library twice a week.

I'm getting better and better. I'm not the odd one out any more. Before it felt as if no one else was finding work hard. I was so confused about that – it was all a mystery – and I was surprised when I started to improve.

I also feel better when I'm cooking, and doing art, Lego® and modelling. At Legoland recently there was a big roomful of Lego and I built a massive Lego zombie model that had a weapon with a spiky thing and entered it for a competition. I was messing around there and went back in and mine was on the stand for the winning entry. Then they called me up on to the stage. I have always loved Lego. You can literally build anything.

Lola, 12, Bedfordshire, England

What makes me feel good about dyslexia is improving in the things I don't think I'm good at. This gives me a real sense of achievement.

I found out I was dyslexic when I was seven, but I didn't know what that was and I wasn't that bothered about it. I think I blamed dyslexia if I didn't understand something. Anything I couldn't do was the fault of the dyslexia.

I had tutors but they kept teaching me different things from what I was learning in school. So they were helpful but not helpful at the same time.

> I blamed dyslexia if I didn't understand something. Anything I couldn't do was the fault of the dyslexia.

I realised that I just needed to keep trying. Now I'm at secondary school my teachers are supportive in English and Maths and they help me out quite a bit.

We asked the maths teacher if she could give me extra support and she did. She gave me extra maths sheets and this has definitely helped. I still struggle with reading but it depends more on the style of the book. I enjoy David Walliams' books and other fun books, but when it comes to serious books I understand them less – though as I get into them I understand them a bit more. Sometimes I think I understand but I am never too sure.

In Maths there are quite a few smart people and quite a few people like me. I concentrate and do the things I can, though I approach some of the work in a different way.

Rory, 17, London, England
'A confusion of words.'

My dad helps me out and he has a lot of different ways to teach me. We do games on the computer.

I am good at sport: football, hockey, netball...any sport really. I'm a fast runner. I can definitely do sport better than I can do academic subjects. I have my mind focused. I really get into them. I have that same focus when I am working on art and designing things. This focus comes naturally to me. This is very different from sitting in a classroom.

Adam, 16, London, England

I think some children are better off not knowing that they are dyslexic. Some use it as an excuse to give up. I have seen that happen to six or seven others. I have watched them take a less competitive path. A lot of people lean back and say, 'I can't do English.' That kind of outlook isn't rewarding in any way. It's a way of avoiding life's challenges.

> I was hounded by the special needs department.
> They were a looming presence, trying to give me spelling books.

I used the benefits that knowing about dyslexia gave me but I also played by the same rules as anyone who didn't have it. I had to work a bit harder but you don't get any rewards for being dyslexic in real life. There are no participation medals.

When I found out I was 12 or 13 and I didn't want to know. I was hounded by the special needs department. They were a looming presence, trying to give me spelling books.

My reading was always much slower and my handwriting was quite rubbish. Those were the two main things. My spelling was quite bad. They said I could use a laptop and that made sense.

I always thought I wasn't good at English or the Humanities but good at Maths and Science and as a result these are the subjects I'm doing now. Giving me extra time was useful and I also had extra time to meet deadlines. I didn't find the laptop helpful. I found it much faster not to use it. The help meant I moved up from a B to an A star in English.

If I spend too much time thinking about what I'm going to write I can't commit to what I've written. I keep trying to perfect it. When I write I speak the words in my head rather than seeing the words and recognising them. That's what slows me down.

11

Support from school

'If you can find the way you learn best you should
be able to learn as well as anybody else.'

Hamish, 15, Stirlingshire, Scotland

I spent a lot of time learning my spellings. Longer than
anyone. Some words I got, and I remembered them, but then
a week afterwards I didn't have a clue. Other words I would
learn the night before and wouldn't be able to spell them on
the day. It was quite a big mixture and I was very frustrated.
I spent so much time trying to memorise those words and
they wouldn't stay. It was just tough.

My handwriting was terrible and punctuation was never
very good so I had extra support and even then I couldn't get
this information into my long-term memory. People began
to notice when I started using IT in class. They were always
asking why I was using it – why I wasn't playing games on it –
but no one was mean.

My mother had asked my teachers about dyslexia in
primary school. They told her they didn't think I had it but

then my brother was being checked and so she sent me down as well. I don't think there was a good understanding of dyslexia when I was young. Some people thought it would just go away.

In high school I learned more about it. Definitely the support from the learning department in my school has been important. They make sure you are comfortable with the way you are learning. I can have scribes for exams and beige paper for printouts. I know some people have had teachers come into class to support them. The school has quite a large department to help you if you are struggling.

Even though school is great at supporting me I just can't get over the memory problem. That's why I didn't take French: I am terrible at it. There are so many things I've had to learn, for instance, in Biology and Chemistry. It's hard to get the facts into your long-term memory. It's frustrating because you feel like you are not performing to the highest level you could be. It feels like you are at a disadvantage.

If you treat dyslexia as the end you are not going to learn.

It is annoying that teachers still question why I am using IT. I try to explain and they say, 'You should be using pen and paper.' I just feel a little bit annoyed. They should understand that this is my way of learning rather than questioning it and making me write, which holds me back. Using beige colours instead of a whiteboard would help too, and giving out digital copies of work.

I struggled a lot when I had pencil and paper. My handwriting is so bad it's tough to read it myself. I'm not embarrassed though. I know I'm good at creative things. I'm quite good at sciences. I enjoy Physics and Applied Maths, I play piano and trombone and I'm taking Music Higher a year early. I think dyslexia has been good for my musical ability. And my brother and uncle are dyslexic and that normalises it for me.

If you treat dyslexia as the end you are not going to learn. If you can find the way you learn best you should be able to learn as well as anybody else. You've just got to try to find your method and get over it. Accept that you will find some things harder than others. You will have to work harder than anyone else and you should overcome it.

Haley, 10, Alabama, USA

In first grade I had trouble reading. I got stuck on words: long words and short words. I was aware other kids were reading quite easily and that made me nervous.

Sometimes I got mad – mostly at home. It was the pressure I felt. I was scared I wouldn't make it through school.

I told my mom and she started trying to figure out why I was struggling. She was looking for reasons. I think she tried to get in touch with teachers. Now they give me help with reading. They try to explain things better. Sometimes I go to a dyslexia class at school and that helps too. The help I received is what has made me feel better. I also have trouble with math and I feel like they could help me out by explaining things better and spending a bit more time with me.

The worst that teachers can do is not help me and pressure me at the same time. When I used to get pressured I would start crying and explain to them that I'm dyslexic. They would get mad at me for crying and I would try hard to stop. That used to happen a lot and sometimes it still does.

Kids don't make fun of me but they do ask questions like, 'Is it hard?' I tell them it's not that hard but it can be frustrating. If other kids with dyslexia are finding the work hard I would tell them it's not that hard for me, to give them hope. Also I like to draw and paint. Dyslexics are really good at art.

> When I used to get pressured I would start crying and explain to them that I'm dyslexic. They would get mad at me for crying and I would try hard to stop.

When I am older I want to be a marine biologist. I like the ocean and I want to learn more about it. I like marine animals as well as other animals. I like learning about the habitats that different animals live in. I am really interested in history, and I'm especially interested in the ocean and all the animals in it.

Nivedhita, 18, Madras, India

I started to realise I was struggling when I was in sixth standard when I was 13. School was very unpleasant. Board copying, marking things in the text, Math and Science were all difficult, and I wasn't good at organising things. I think the other children noticed because they used to criticise and laugh at me.

I moved school and going to school is now really pleasant and enjoyable. Because of my experiences I know that the best thing a teacher can do for children with dyslexia is to give them extra care and attention – and they should also educate the other children in the class regarding this. They shouldn't scold children with dyslexia or show irritation towards them.

All through my schooling my mother was helping and supporting me. Parents need to have immense patience. They can make their child realise that she has a problem and deal with it – if they can give the child the opportunity to learn in the right environment, bringing out the strengths of the child, and allowing the child to employ coping strategies.

This will help boost the child's self-confidence and help them become a well-rounded personality, facing life as an independent individual.

I am good at cooking, housekeeping and, in academics I'm particularly good at Social Science. I love jewellery-making and my mother and grandmother are helping me with designs.

I should now go on to higher studies and equip myself to earn a living. I am aware of my strengths and needs. I have been given the right opportunities from my childhood so I am not scared to face the world anymore. I can handle any situation boldly since I have been moulded to face challenges right from my childhood.

Abby, 10, Illinois, USA

I like being special and getting a lot of attention from the teachers. My mom and the principal at school have helped me most. My mom is the one who found out I was dyslexic. She's the one who gets me all the help and she's really good at that. The principal understands what I need to help me understand. And my friends are supportive of me. Once my class was reading a book with so many big words that I couldn't read them and I was so confused. I had no idea what the class was doing. Two of my friends came over and we read the book together and they helped me sound out the words I couldn't read on my own.

Abby, 10, Illinois, USA
'My strength.'

I found out I was dyslexic in second grade when I was eight. Before this, I didn't really know what I was, but I knew I was struggling, mostly with reading and spelling. My math is not the best. It's usually hard. I was frustrated that other people knew how to do their schoolwork and I didn't, and I went to a lot of teachers for more help.

> I was frustrated that other people knew how to do their schoolwork and I didn't, and I went to a lot of teachers for more help.

Now I do better at school. They know how to help me and I have a good teacher, a computer, an iPad and more support. I have got better at reading. I like to read mysteries and funny books. I especially love the book *I Funny*.

I'm good at soccer and sports and I want to be a soccer player. I'm very good at being aware of the field and anticipating what's happening. This helps me to run at the right angle to get the ball. I think maybe that's to do with being dyslexic and knowing what's going on around me.

Nick, 18, Norfolk, England

My dyslexia wasn't diagnosed until last year. An educational psychologist said I had been compensating. Most of my IQ tests were in a high percentile and I was putting 120 per cent of effort into everything. That's why I managed for so long. I had always been told that dyslexia meant letters were jumbling about the page and that's not true for me. I can read, but if I read for a long time, it's like tensing a muscle. It's quite strenuous.

The best thing that happened to me was changing schools. I was going to do Physics, Maths and Economics and this might have been the worst choice. I don't think I have as much of a science brain as I thought I did. Instead I did a series of tests that told me what I should do – English, Economics and Politics – and this was quite eye-opening.

I had been to a state school but I switched to private school for A levels. I don't want to critique what I had before, but the resources there were spread too thin. At private school you get what you pay for. It's more focused.

Private school kids like their cliques and I did find them very cliquey, but I broke through. All was good.

If I hadn't changed schools I would never have found out I was dyslexic. I was under the impression that reading and numbers were as difficult for everyone else. I was on the borderline and I didn't think there was anything wrong. There are a large number of students who don't have the opportunities I had and won't be able to realise their full potential under the education system, which is very frustrating.

> If I hadn't changed schools I would never have found out I was dyslexic. I was under the impression that reading and numbers were as difficult for everyone else.

The things that indicated I might have dyslexia were the aptitude tests. I had always scored at the top. Whenever my report cards would come in my parents would see my results and be saying, 'We know that you can do better.' That's why they wanted to switch to a school where I received more attention.

If you have dyslexia I think one of the most important things is to know that you've got a unique mind. I think dyslexia really brings something extra to the world and a different perspective. The way people with dyslexia think is different. I look at my dad. I don't think he's diagnosed but his approach to difficult tasks always astounds my mum. Dyslexia is a strength and should not be seen as a weakness.

Scott, 13, County Offaly, Ireland

The worst thing a teacher can do is to give you lots of homework when you don't know how to do it. This is not great. I would do a bit and then wouldn't be able to do any more. The other worst thing is getting you to read out in class. I'd be sitting there, seeing the words and

> Asking for help is the best thing anyone with dyslexia can do.

wouldn't get any of them. Some of the others would laugh. One teacher was tough on me and I still wasn't able to read. I sat at the table and shut down and then the tears would come. I couldn't cope with it.

Three others in the class had been diagnosed but I hadn't been. My mam had talked to two teachers before and they had said no, they didn't think I was dyslexic. Then she said it to the primary school principal and I was put down for testing, which was funded by the school. This was a great help to my family.

I have found Irish and spellings hard and I have a poor memory, though I'm not too bad at maths. Secondary school is much better. I have been pulled out of languages: Irish, German and French.

Now I have been told I am dyslexic I get more help. I go into different classes and do more reading and spelling. That's what teachers should do. Just help us and spend more time with us. Asking for help is the best thing anyone with dyslexia can do. When you get help you can do your homework.

Gilbert, 10, Texas, USA

When I was young I couldn't read very well. I was always mixing up my b's and d's. I felt sad about it. Even though I got help I carried on finding school hard and I still do. I think this means that I should practice more. What helps me most is coming to the dyslexia class. I don't mix up my letters so often now.

> It's really important that teachers help kids more often.

It's really important that teachers help kids more often. The worst thing they can do is not help. Moms and Dads should read to their kids – that's what would help them the most. It would help them to understand.

I would say to someone with dyslexia who was struggling that they can do it. If you are dyslexic you are special. All you need to do is to practice a little bit more.

Corinne, 17, Bedfordshire, England

What has helped me most are my sessions with the academic support teacher. She helps me find ways I can revise. I am studying Music and she showed me how to use colours to link different sections on the sheets of music. There is so much to remember when you read music and the colours match up to the melody and the harmony. The melody is in one colour, the harmony in another. Without the colours I would be struggling a lot more.

I love music. I do violin and oboe and I recently was given a merit in grade eight. I know that I will keep using the techniques when I leave school.

I also like visual, creative things and when I leave school I want to do archaeology at university. It's very hands-on. You can touch everything. You get to see little fingerprints in clay and pottery. Some of music is hands-on too, such as composition and performances.

For other subjects I have been taught another technique. We use a whiteboard. We read words and then rub one of them off. Then we have to remember what the word was that was rubbed off. Then another word is rubbed off and you have to remember that. You end up reading an empty whiteboard but you have repeated what was there so often you remember it. I've found that when words are rubbed out you can still visualise them being there.

When I came to this school I was struggling with reading and spelling and I've been given help with them. They still bother me now but I've been shown ways to make them easier. I've worked out ways to deal with mental maths. I write everything down and find long ways to work out the answers. I still can't spell very well and I prefer to type rather than write by hand when I'm doing homework. This means I can add in words where I forget to include them.

Edward, 9, Powys, Wales

My old school was quite nice until it got to Year 2. Then the teacher started to get stricter. If you didn't do a certain amount of work you had to miss your break. I wasn't a very quick writer so I would miss half my lunch break. It was impossible for me to do the work.

I thought this was unfair as I was doing my best. For me the problem wasn't so much my spellings but my handwriting. I couldn't move my hand that fast. I used to get a bit bullied because I was quite slow and I remember in running games people used to tease me.

I moved school and the new school was great from the beginning. You don't miss breaks – unless you only wrote two words in an hour. Straight away I thought the teachers were a lot nicer, a lot less strict and they were funnier. I'm happy to go into school now.

My reading has improved, I'm a bit more confident, and I have got neater and quicker in my writing.

I only properly got told about dyslexia recently. I have just started to go to a little school once a week to help me with my work, and that is helping me too.

Tristan, 9, Mississippi, USA

The worst thing a teacher can do is send a child home. Children don't want to be bad kids. I get a little angry at school. Our class gets a little loud and it gives me a headache and then I get angry.

I don't get good results, but for me reading is the worst thing. When they do reading tests at school then I mostly can't read in front of other people. I don't know what the words say, especially shorter words.

The best thing about school is going out at recess and playing with my friends. Also I am good at math; I'm good at sport and good at drawing. I have a teacher that helps me and other kids with reading at school and my mom helps me with spellings and homework. I like hanging out with my friends and they like to help me too.

The teacher who helps with dyslexia is really nice to us and my other teacher is nice too. I only get angry when my medicine for ADHD [Attention Deficit Hyperactivity Disorder] starts to wear off. Then I start to get a little wild. I start to get frustrated and a little hyper. I don't feel happy in class so I say stuff in my head to try to calm myself down. I always want to be nice and kind.

They knew I was dyslexic because the numbers go backwards when I write them. My daddy and my brother are dyslexic too. My daddy said he didn't know the word 'study' when he was nine and I knew it when I was eight. We have tests coming up and I want to move to the next grade so I'm working real hard.

Corie, 12, Merthyr Tydfil, Wales

I have dyslexia and also ADHD and autism. In the infants I found work a bit easier but in the juniors I found it much harder. I do a lot of work with the SpLD (Specific Learning Difficulties) teacher and my spelling, reading and writing are improving. My problem now is mainly with maths. My SpLD teacher explains things in a simpler way and, because it is a small group, it isn't too loud when someone answers her.

My concentration is not very good because I was bullied in the infants. Some of it was about being autistic and some was about liking trains. I didn't tell Mam and Dad until Year 6.

In Year 5, when I was ten, I got angry and kicked off. In Year 6 I shouted to everyone in the class that I couldn't take it anymore. People were annoying me. My teacher came in and told me not to misbehave, but then the headmistress came in and calmed me down because she knew me.

My SpLD teacher also teaches mindfulness. This helps me concentrate and calm down, and it even helps me sleep.

I'm good at writing stories. I have a really good imagination. I like writing about adventures and anything that involves trains. I like the way trains work – the way they have evolved from being simple machines to highly complex ones. I'd like to be a train driver when I'm older.

I used to watch *Thomas the Tank Engine* when I was young and some of my stories are based on that. Another story was about a train driver driving his train away from a storm. I am good at thinking of ideas. I find that if a group of other people are thinking of ideas they tend to be more or less the same, but I think of some that are completely different.

Matthew, 10, Texas, USA

Sometimes, when I'm reading, my mind goes away from the book. I don't focus properly and I start thinking about something else. I'm not good at reading really, but I'm good at math.

I try hard to make sure my writing looks good so the teachers can read it, but I know I need to work harder to make sure. I'm getting better. Teachers should really help kids who have dyslexia. When I get help, this means I can see what the question is and what it is talking about. If the teachers don't pay attention to kids with dyslexia, that is not going to help them.

I still find it difficult to keep focused but I try very hard. I want to say to kids with dyslexia, 'You can do it. Just believe in yourself.'

Oscar, 11, Merthyr Tydfil, Wales

I didn't notice that I was dyslexic but my dyslexia teacher told me there was a discrepancy between my overall ability and my reading which are good and my spelling which isn't so good. My English teacher had noticed this and told her.

When you get older and you get a job if you spell something wrong the manager might try to say, 'What are you doing here?'

Oscar, 11, Merthyr Tydfil, Wales
'Boy writing at his desk.'

I now go to lessons with Mrs Cooksey who helps people with dyslexia at school. It's a small class and that means she's focusing on the small group instead of a bigger group. It helps me to learn spelling rules and spelling patterns, like when to use 'k 'or 'ck' or 'c'. I definitely feel better about my spelling now. I can tell when a spelling is right but it's just remembering them.

I know that in exams you can get low marks just because you have problems with your spelling. I should do well in my exams but I'm worried that the spelling aspect might stop that because there are new changes in the marking system. I want to be an artist or an architect when I leave school. What I like about art is that I get to express my emotions through drawing roses, cars, people or bottles of water. Anything.

Kendall, 11, Texas, USA

I couldn't read and write well when I was in third grade and I felt really bad that I couldn't do it. I looked around and saw they could do it better than me. I told my mom and she said she would find me a class that would help me to read those words and she put me in a dyslexia class. I didn't know what dyslexia was and I felt a little bit scared that I had it.

> The letters were still jumping but I read correctly and I'm much more confident now.

Then I began to understand and I felt a little bit better. At the dyslexia class, they showed me how to do cursive handwriting with the letters joined together. I was surprised that my writing got better. My reading got better too. Before this the letters were jumping everywhere. The letters were still jumping but I read correctly and I'm much more confident now. I read *Dracula* by myself over spring break after my teacher introduced me to the book. I want to read some more horror stories. They're scary and they've got blood! It's my dream to write my own horror story. Sometimes it would be less scary and then, suddenly, it would get more scary. I would illustrate it because I like to draw a lot. I like to show my drawings to everybody else and give them to people who are nice to me, who are friends with me and who care about me.

Teachers should help with reading and writing and it would be bad if a teacher just didn't care and just helped the other kids who didn't have dyslexia.

I know now that by practising my words and believing in myself my work gets better. If someone tells me I can't do it I don't pay attention to them. If you have dyslexia you can do this and you can get better.

Damien, 11, Texas, USA

In second grade I was a bit slow with reading and writing. No one was mean to me about it. One thing I'm really good at is making friends easily – just being friendly – so people were nice to me and I was nice to them.

When I started going to dyslexia class they would help me a lot. We did cursive, the writing when you connect the letters, and that made things much better.

> The best thing a mom and dad could do, if they have a kid with dyslexia, is to take them to the library.

The best thing a mom and dad could do, if they have a kid with dyslexia, is to take them to the library. That will help them to know about books. Teachers must pay attention to them and help them more.

12

Support from outside school

'My sister is not dyslexic and she helps me a lot with everything.'

Evelyne, 17, County Whitlow, Ireland

When my family understood that I was dyslexic, they really went out of their way to make life easier for me.

I wasn't diagnosed until I was 15. Before this I had no idea what dyslexia was. No one had ever talked about it or suggested I might have it. I had thought that there was something wrong with me or that I was stupid. Everyone else seemed to grasp things easily and I was just not getting it.

I can remember back to being about eight and we were getting on to more difficult topics at school. I was trying to subtract and to tackle new spellings and I just couldn't do them. Everyone else was fine and I didn't know what was going on. No teacher said anything to me. My reading was just a little bit slow and it had taken me longer to learn to read.

I didn't tell Mum and Dad then. I had no idea that dyslexia was a thing and I was honestly a bit embarrassed. I made the decision to hold it all to myself. I let my parents read to me and I didn't read to them.

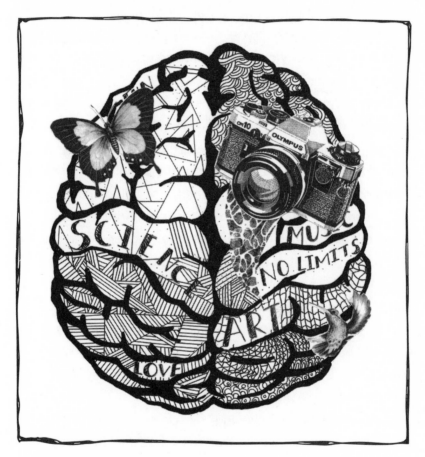

Evelyne, 17, County Whitlow, Ireland

I think I managed to hide what was going on quite well. I never let the other kids hear me read. I asked the teachers not to ask me and they just thought I was shy.

All of this put me at a distance from my friends. After all, if I wasn't talking they weren't going to get to know me. It excluded me a bit from everyone else, but I thought it was better than them finding out.

On the bright side, I was always good at art. This was the one thing. The teacher would always pick me to draw things and the other kids would say, 'That's so good.' This made me feel a bit better.

When I went into secondary school in Ireland things went downhill further. Everything was harder and all my friends were grasping lessons a lot better. The teachers thought I was lazy. I really found English and German difficult. I used to pretend to be sick and go to the nurse so I didn't have to go to lessons as they were so embarrassing for me. We had to read out loud and, if we had a test, the teacher would call out the scores in front of everyone. I just thought, 'Someone help me.' It was all so public and showed how far behind I was and that there might be a problem.

I would spend these moments on the verge of tears. I would be sweating and so embarrassed. I felt completely apart from the rest of the class and I was sure they would be talking about me afterwards.

I dreaded parents' evenings. Teachers would say, 'She's very polite but she doesn't work very hard' or, 'She's so behind the average.' My parents would come home and report this back. It's not helpful to your self-esteem. My sister found school so easy and I felt as if I'd let them down. My parents are lovely. It wasn't their fault that they hadn't heard of dyslexia. They didn't think I was being lazy, they just thought I was a bit behind. My spelling was awful so I don't know why the teachers didn't pick it up.

Before school I would sit and cry. I just didn't feel I belonged. School was a minefield. Sometimes I would be calm and get comfortable with a topic; moments later there would be confusion and chaos. There were sickies, a lot of sickies. Always something that couldn't be proven like a migraine.

Luckily for me I am close to my sister. I told her how far behind I was and it was she who suggested I might be dyslexic. Having heard my story, my mum is convinced that she is dyslexic as well and spent her school days without any help.

> School was a minefield. Sometimes I would be calm and get comfortable with a topic; moments later there would be confusion and chaos.

When my sister suggested dyslexia, I thought for the first time that maybe there was a reason for everything I was going through. My parents were quite open to the idea and talked to the learning support teacher in my school who gave them a name where I was sent for testing. Half of me thought, 'I hope I have a reason for being like this.' The other half thought, 'I hope I don't have it because if I do, then what?' But when the educational psychologist told me about the dyslexia it was a relief. There was an explanation for why I was so behind my classmates. I didn't just feel stupid any more.

After this the school helped, though it was a bit too late. They offered some resource classes but I couldn't have them because they ran at the same time as my Irish lessons. School felt that Irish was more important. I felt that I couldn't grasp English so why was I trying to grasp Irish? It just wasn't going to work.

I still struggle now. I either get on terribly in a subject or really well. This year, Science went really well, Maths was great, English not well, Irish not well, History and Geography not very good, Art was good. I wasn't expecting good results in the subjects I did badly in but I was happy with the other results – the ones that matter to me. They are the ones that make me feel good.

Where things go wrong is that we would be covering a particular topic and we would have been working on it for a while. Finally I would start to feel confident about it. Then a teacher moves on to the next topic and all my confidence goes because I find myself in this tremendous struggle again, trying to play catch-up with my peers.

This year we have the leaving certificate. I have new Science subjects that I love and have done well in. I don't have to do History or Geography. For English the novel we have to do is *Emma* by Jane Austen, which is 55 chapters long and I can barely read. I see a lot of white lines and the words move a little bit too much for me. I get so scared of reading that I don't remember much of what I read at all.

My friendships have continued to suffer. Half of my friendship group are high achievers. Sometimes I feel angry at them or frustrated about how easy they have it. Of course they don't have it easy but for me it feels like that. I can't help myself.

No one else in the class is dyslexic but I wanted the challenge of higher level. There are accommodations for people with dyslexia. I'm definitely going to apply for them. My school is not helpful so I will have to do this for myself, though it's hard to get these without the school backing me.

When I leave, I'd love to be a nurse or a science teacher. I think I'd be a good teacher. I certainly would understand children who have dyslexia. I would help them to realise there isn't anything wrong with them. I'd make sure they knew that it's actually better to tell someone you have dyslexia. This also helps them understand themselves better.

Teachers should also support you and make sure you don't feel like you are stupid. They should maybe tell other people in the class to be nicer to children with dyslexia and not go on about test results and how easy subjects are, because they are certainly not easy for everyone!

Joe G, 15, Bedfordshire, England

When I was younger I hated the thought of the stereotype of someone with dyslexia: people thinking you're going to be stupid or not as smart as others are. I would always hide it a bit and certainly wasn't open about it. I realise now that dyslexia doesn't have anything to do with how clever I am. It's just how my mind works.

Both my parents are supportive of me but, more than anything else, I think what my mum does has helped. She is on my side. She reads a lot about dyslexia so she can understand how I think.

A teacher once wrote on my book that I needed to learn to copy off the board properly and write the words down exactly as she has written them. This was something I had always struggled with. My mum emailed the teacher and said, 'He tries to do this but his mind works in a different way.' The next day the teacher apologised and said, 'It had slipped my mind that you were dyslexic.'

I found out about the dyslexia when I was seven. I had always found it difficult to remember things because my memory was always a bit off. In English I would forget a lot. When I was reading I would struggle to read the words. My dad would say, 'Stop jumping from one word to another.' The teacher asked my mum if she wanted to get me tested and the results said I was severely dyslexic. My mum looked into it. No one in the family is dyslexic. The symptoms were a lot worse than she expected. If she tells me four things I only remember one of them.

When I was a younger reader I would have a book and get half way down the first page and click back in my mind. I would end up on another page, not remembering what I had read. My mind would jump to a conclusion. How it got from one bit to another I have no idea. My maths was always good – my numbers have always been better than my letters.

Recently I have got into Chemistry and Physics. It's the physical subjects I like to do and I like these because something has to happen. That's why I want to go into engineering. In English there isn't even a set answer. If I had a job sitting in a cubicle and typing, my mind would wander. With engineering I would be kept busy and that would help.

I think that, weirdly, dyslexia has benefits for me. Although my memory is not good I can remember certain facts. I won't remember what I had for tea a few days ago but I will remember what somebody said to me.

If I'm trying to visualise something, I can put it together in my mind so I know what it's going to look like before I get it down on paper. I know it's going to work. It's a little bit like if I see a picture of something, I try to think about how it goes together. I remember this by thinking of a finger joint. When I think of a finger joint in 3D that helps me to know how I would make it.

Grainne, 12, County Cork, Ireland

There were phases I went through of not wanting to be me because I was dyslexic, I felt I wasn't good enough. Then Breda, my mum, would tell me, 'It's a gift in some ways.' Knowing this really helps me and I feel it actually is now. One of the days I felt really down we made a big long list of things I could do that I hadn't been able to do when I was young, all sorts of things such as surfing and rock climbing.

> From not being able to read, I tried again and I was able to. I was overwhelmed by shock and happiness.

I know that Breda was worried when I was five or six because I was falling behind everyone else at school. I remember not being able to read like the others or write down the questions or spellings. I went to see someone and she said I was dyslexic.

I felt almost angry at myself because I couldn't do the schoolwork. The rest of the time I didn't know what to feel because I didn't know what was going on; maybe sad that I wasn't up to scratch with the other kids.

Every day I went to school thinking everything would be all right when I got home. Then Breda suddenly asked me if I would like to be home-schooled. I didn't really want to go to school but then I was also afraid of not going to school. The fear of not having any friends was a lot of pressure.

Grainne, 12, County Cork, Ireland

As soon as I started working at home I picked up so much progress. I'm now able to read books and my spelling is a bit better. I think I needed my own time to learn these things. At school they were just shovelling it all at me and I didn't know what to do with all the information. I became more and more confused and I soldiered on.

At school I remember once a day I would go down to this girl teacher and she would help me with my spellings and do it in fun ways and she gave me stuff to write down. We did that but it was always hard and it didn't help that much. I felt I was letting everyone down because I couldn't keep up.

I have been home-schooled for about three or four years now. I wasn't concerned that my mum wouldn't know what to do. Her mum was a teacher and her perspective is that kids do learn and will pick it up. She started bringing learning into our daily lives. If I had to get something from the shops she would give me a certain amount of coins to count out. That would help me for my maths.

I still have some little person in me who feels I should know it all already. The other part of me is saying, 'I don't know this. All the more reason for me to learn it now.'

From not being able to read, I tried again and I was able to. I was overwhelmed by shock and happiness. A strange feeling. It could have been because I was no longer anxious. It could have been that I just needed to do it in my own time.

I'm thinking of going to secondary school now I can read, just to try it out. I do like the idea of going to school. It's just the idea of being really pressurised to do so much stuff in so much time that I don't like. I would both love to go and I'm afraid of going there.

I like art, surfing, snorkelling and dance. These are what I feel I am most good at. My best friend goes to some of the dance classes I go to. I would like to be a dancer when I leave school. The way my mother taught me angles in maths was by showing me 360 degrees and 180 degrees during a spin while I danced. If I go to surf camp we talk about 360 degree turns so this help me with the entire process of learning and makes it more fun.

The worst thing a parent can do is force their children to do something that they don't feel comfortable doing. I felt weak in school. The worst thing for me would to have been forced to stay there and that's why my mum took me out. On the other hand, some kids really love going to school.

Learning when you have dyslexia is difficult in some ways and fun in others. I still have some little person in me who feels I should know it all already. The other part of me is saying, 'I don't know this. All the more reason for me to learn it now.' Some things are just not easy. I would never be able to read the time properly with a digital clock. I have a watch and on it the one is a 13. What! You couldn't make it more complicated.

Harriet, 10, Victoria, Australia

My mum told me I had dyslexia – she found it out. My old school kept telling me, 'Don't do that, don't do this.' They didn't do anything. They didn't even believe in dyslexia. They just told me to work harder like the other kids. My problems are mostly in reading, writing and spelling. Spelling is pretty hard. Irregular words – what?!

Three or four times I had to read out in front of the class. I got really scared and didn't want to do it. They were all looking. I got nervous and my hands would start shaking. I had to do it. I had to. They didn't help me and I got it wrong. I felt disappointed and a bit sad that I couldn't do it and they could.

In the end I got moved to a different school where they helped me a lot. Maths is pretty tricky now I'm in grade four, so my teacher's helping me but it's difficult. It feels like the others can all do it and I can't and that's unfair.

Harriet, 10, Victoria, Australia
'Me and my mum.'

My best friend and her mum are great. She's still my best friend even though I moved schools and I was anxious about it. Now I'm glad I did. At my old school they didn't explain stuff. At the new school they explain things well. I get extra help from my mum because she is the learning support teacher there.

Now I feel I'm on track and I can do the work the way the others do it. I know I can just ask for help whenever I need it.

We did a special thing at school where kids with dyslexia came up to the front of the school and talked about it if they wanted to. There are quite a few of us. I remember at my old school I felt sad and now I feel happy.

I'm good at other stuff. I love everything about art and I do art class after school. I know I'm getting good. I might like to be an art teacher when I leave school. I also want to look after two kids from the orphanage. It's hard to get homes for them. And I want three golden retrievers. I thought it might be nice for them to get a home.

The best thing if you have dyslexia is when they help you a lot with everything, helping and not criticising if you're not getting good. My sister is eight and she is not dyslexic. She helps me a lot with everything. She's just like a twin. Sometimes I say words wrong and she corrects me or she helps me spell a word if I don't know how to spell it.

It's really hard if you have dyslexia, but keep going and you will be able to do it in the end. I like school now. I do find it hard but I still like it. In the holidays my mum runs this camp for kids with dyslexia. We go over stuff we learnt at school to make sure it went into our memories and do fun stuff in the afternoon. Really cool stuff. I just sometimes say to myself, 'You can do it, you can do it. You can.'

Lucy, 15, Stirlingshire, Scotland

I'm told quite a lot that people with dyslexia are better at creative and practical things. I do love and enjoy these. I do music, drawing, skateboarding and ice skating. This helps me forget the other stuff. I'm out, I'm relaxing my brain, I'm focused and not thinking about what I have to do at school.

I am a carer for my dad. I tend to put others before me and people do think they can talk to me. I think, because of the struggles I have had, I have learnt to look after others if anyone is making fun of them or ridiculing them, making them feel stupid or dumb.

Lucy, 15, Stirlingshire, Scotland
'Self-portrait with art and music.'

Being dyslexic gives me hope and inspiration. It makes me think I can do something. It makes me want to try harder and do the best I can. Sometimes I am jealous because of what other people can do, but mainly I am inspired by them.

My mum realised I was dyslexic when I was in primary school and they didn't do anything. Then, in the first year of high school, they sorted it straight away. Reading was the main problem. I've never been good at taking in information and helping it stay in my brain. If I have to try to learn a poem

I get someone to read it to me and then I read it myself. I will remember it for 15 minutes and then I can't remember the first line. As I go up the levels at school I have more to remember and then it gets harder to understand and that makes it worse.

School says that's not because of dyslexia but I think that's not true and I have been on the phone to Dyslexia Scotland for advice. Nothing stays in my brain.

I have learnt to do the best I can and deal with it. One of my friends has that feeling that she's useless and isn't going to get any better. She was doing the very best she could and was breaking down in tears because of one teacher. I don't think that teacher is there any more. It was terrible. The worst thing to witness. Teachers should just support people and if they need help, help them. They need to be understanding of the situation.

Dyslexia Scotland has helped me a lot, and school, and my mum. She's the main person who helps me. She tries to find ways for me to learn things. She got me coloured lenses and has done all she can to get the school to recognise it – not just for me, but for others as well.

Charlotte, 9, County Dublin, Ireland

I go to a dyslexia workshop and that helps me. I do reading, worksheets and use a computer there. I use something called Word Check and I have to figure out what the words are.

The workshop is for two hours on a Wednesday night and I love that all these others there have dyslexia and I'm not alone. I'm not different.

Charlotte, 9, County Dublin, Ireland
'Fox alphabet.'

Before, when I went to school, I was in tears and my mum was in tears. Homework was taking four times longer than it should. Now I have been diagnosed, I find school easier and I get support in different ways. The main thing is my confidence has improved. It had just been knocked down so far and now it is getting built up again.

We realised about the dyslexia when I was seven. I found writing stuff down hard, and remembering stuff, and maths was hard too. Now I have a great teacher. The school has extra teachers and I get support. If we're doing maths I go out with a few other people and get taught in a smaller group. If there's spellings, I do different spellings – I do that with other people as well.

Before I realised I had dyslexia I found school very difficult. When I found out it made sense of things. I like animals and would like to be a vet. I like drawing animals too. I drew an owl last week with pastels and people said it was really good.

Veena, 15, Madras, India

School was hell for me. I didn't want to go. I realised I was struggling when I was ten and memorising, writing, identifying questions and writing answers in exams were all difficult for me. No one helped me in school. I noticed the other children were finding things easier and was wondering how they did that. They noticed that I was finding studying hard.

> I went to a new school after this help and hell changed into heaven.

Then I went to a special school and got remedial help and that changed things. I went to a new school after this help and hell changed into heaven. Now I am the class monitor!

I am good at singing and badminton and get lots of prizes. It is the singing that made me feel better about being dyslexic. I represent my school at state level.

I want to become a civil servant, which is one of the highest positions in the government. I would like to serve my country.

Teachers should always identify people with dyslexia in their classes and help them. They should never scold you and compare you with other children.

And parents should always support their children, like my mom always helps me.

Olivia, 10, Victoria, Australia

The worst thing at school is when they get you to read out loud. I'm really nervous and because I'm dyslexic I find it really embarrassing how I would slip on words. My teacher doesn't get me to do that but if we have another teacher who doesn't know me, they ask me to. When that happens I feel really embarrassed and think people are going to make fun of me. I do worry about that. Most of my friends know I am dyslexic, so sometimes I sit next to them and they might help me on a couple of things.

In grade one when I was six I was struggling in spelling and reading out words. It was a bit bad but then I can't do anything about it because I was born with it. It was kind of a good thing when I was told I had dyslexia because then I knew I had to improve in some things.

It was a little bit strange when the other children didn't struggle with reading and spelling but my teacher helped me, and Nathalie, who's my tutor, and my mum.

I think Nathalie has helped me the most. We keep going over stuff that we need to improve. She helps me learn it in a way that I understand. It's a different way of learning from the way that people who aren't dyslexic learn. She helps with word connections and sounds.

Probably the best thing for me is that I'm getting so much help. I know what I need to improve on. I feel proud of myself that I have learnt some words that will help me with my spelling.

Olivia, 10, Victoria, Australia
'My tutor Nathalie, Mum and me.'

The teachers help me. If I have my hand up and I say I don't understand they might read it over to me and explain in a way that helps. In the past I didn't know what to do when

I didn't understand. I was frightened to put my hand up because I wasn't sure what was going on. It's a relief that now I know.

Dyslexia doesn't mean you're not good at anything. I'm really good at sport and maths. I love drawing and colouring and art. I kind of want to be a kindergarten teacher because I love little kids. They are so cute.

Dyslexia means that I have a little glitch so I need to be taught differently to others. I don't feel different because I have lots of friends. I love going to school.

Callum, 12, County Dublin, Ireland

I just get on with things and I don't really worry about them. If there's a subject in school I don't like, I try to make it fun or less boring. I'm a positive person and my friends are very positive people too. It's a good way to be if you're dyslexic.

I'm really good at making stuff with my hands, like using Lego® to create vehicles and buildings, I also love making model aeroplanes. When I go to secondary school, I will do woodwork and art, I'm looking forward to that. I think I might be a woodwork teacher when I'm older or maybe an engineer like my dad. I hope to work with my granddad on his farm when I'm a teenager, driving and fixing the farm machinery.

I go to a workshop every week for dyslexic kids. That's the best thing about being dyslexic at my age. At the workshop I really enjoy being with my friends. We all sort of think we are different from the other kids in school, but we all have different forms of dyslexia so we all have one thing in common at the workshop. We think being dyslexic is a good thing.

There are 25 of us at the workshop with four teachers. We do activities and practise writing and reading. We do some work on the computer and play games together. Ever since I started going there I have found it has improved my reading a lot.

I recently took part in a research programme at Dublin City University. They were examining the front part of my brain and were testing it to see if it could be retrained to improve my ability to read. I had to carry out tasks on a computer while wearing a skull cap with sensors on it, to monitor my brain activity. I also had to spend two months doing online tests at home. I liked being part of a scientific discovery project.

I was eight years old when I found out I had dyslexia. My teacher had a meeting with my parents and I was sent to do some tests. Once I found out, I suddenly understood why I found reading so difficult compared to my friends, and it felt good to know there was a reason.

I tried to learn Irish but I found it very difficult learning two languages. My mum told me I had to stop doing Irish and focus on English and I was okay with that. One of my friends in my class is dyslexic as well, and instead of doing Irish, we sit together and finish other work and listen to a CD of instrumental music.

I enjoy reading now and I'm okay with Maths. It's not my favourite subject but I like percentages. My writing could be a bit better. I had a teacher last year who let me use a fountain pen and I found it really easy to write with. Sometimes I forget to use commas and full stops. Sometimes I use the wrong letters when I'm writing and don't spell things properly, but my teacher knows what I'm trying to say.

I like riding my BMX bike and doing tricks with it. I also like playing golf, sailing, Gaelic football, hurling and Olympic handball. I love being outdoors on my bike and playing sport. It's much more fun than being in the classroom, but I do like art and science projects – those are the best part of the school day for me.

Lydia, 8, Georgia, USA

The hardest year for me was last year because I find spelling big words really hard. My reading is a lot better now I have a good tutor. She makes things fun.

She gets a bucket and a bunch of sticks. Some of the sticks have words on them and a few say 'bam'. I have to pull the sticks out of the bucket and say the words. If the stick says 'bam' I have to put all the sticks in and start again. That's just one of the games she does.

My handwriting is good. Math is probably one of my favourite things to learn. I like when people read books to me and I like art and painting. I play with MagnaTiles® and plastic blocks and build things with them.

I see my tutor twice a week and my mom teaches me at home. I like being home a lot. I used to cry when I had to go to kindergarten. We were late to school almost every day because I didn't want to go, even though I only went for half a day. Then after school there was homework. It took a long time and it was all the things I was struggling with. It should have taken ten minutes but it took 45.

I have learned to read in the last few months and my mom gets me to read books aloud. We play games together too. Making learning fun is the best thing a teacher can do. I think it would be harder if I went back to school.

When I am grown up I want to take care of pets or be a veterinarian or a dog sitter. We have a dog called Penny and she keeps me company in the day. We have 11 chickens and I was allowed to give the chickens names. Some of them are Frosting, Sprinkles, Starburst, Star, Snow and Buttercup. I like the animals because they are cute. I talk to the chickens, hold them, feed them and gather the eggs. You can tell from the colour of the egg which chicken laid them. We have some eggs that are greenish blue, some are brown and some are white. I like to cook with them and make scrambled eggs and chocolate chip pancakes.

Lachlan, 11, Victoria, Australia

In grade three, when I was nine, I thought I wasn't doing that well. I couldn't spell most words and was having trouble reading. I would rely on pictures in the books to help me guess what the words were. I knew the pictures had to match the story and make sense – but that system couldn't last forever.

I was a little overwhelmed by schoolwork and couldn't get through it all. Some other people were struggling but no one as bad as I was. My parents asked the school to test me and they kept saying, 'It's all going to click next year.' There was a long waiting list for public testing so Mum and Dad decided to go private. We went down to SPELD, an organisation that helps kids with dyslexia, to get a test and I got diagnosed.

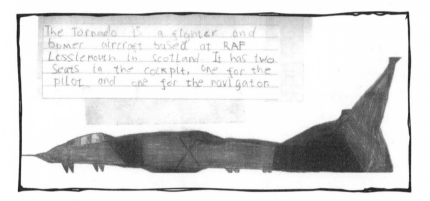

The Tornado is a fighter and bomer aircraft based at RAF Lossiemouth In Scotland. It has two seats in the cockpit, one for the pilot and one for the navigator.

Callum, 8, County Dublin, Ireland

We were driving home after my day of testing and my mum asked me if I was okay with being told I was dyslexic. I said to her that it sounded like a label; it didn't feel like me. Now I see it is not a negative thing. It's just that I learn in a different way.

Mum got me a tutor and she helped me get back on track. Since then I have been doing pretty well. She's helped me with my spelling, maths and reading. I guess she helps because it's more one-on-one. If I give an answer I'm not going to get flustered that everyone else is listening to me.

No one is teasing me. Being separated from everyone is what makes the difference.

When I was told I had dyslexia I knew there was a reason I was getting behind. I wasn't a person doing something wrong. I wasn't dumb. The other kids at school were encouraging and were helping me a lot more.

> ...my mum asked me if I was okay with being told I was dyslexic. I said to her that it sounded like a label; it didn't feel like me.

A lot of the time at school they put you on a time limit for work. For me that's hard because I have to think of my answers before I can put them down and I have to spell them out. Thanks to the help I've had I can now do this in the time limit.

Sometimes my teacher sits down and helps me when everyone else is working. I can feel that the spotlight's on me but, if it's helping me, we have got to do it. The best thing they can do is help you. I am very determined to do well.

I think my visual side is a lot stronger. Having dyslexia is okay because all the help you can get is there if you tell someone about it. I had a good experience with the way my friends reacted. If I hadn't had the support I would be more overwhelmed by what I can't do. The things I have to do would all be piling up.

Sonny, 13, Buckinghamshire, England

My sister was diagnosed with dyslexia when I was a kid and my mum noticed I had the same problems. That's how they found out about me. I think because my sister had it I thought it was fine. It was normal. I knew about it already.

I was having trouble reading and writing. I wasn't mad on it. When I was reading I had these problems with the words. They didn't make sense. I just went to school and tried. I didn't enjoy most lessons. Every time I woke up it was like, 'Oh...school.'

I like PE, ICT, Drama and Art. I don't mind Maths that much but I don't enjoy English. In my secondary school in some classes I'm with groups of 30 and I don't understand what the teachers are meaning. When I ask, it makes a little more sense but I still don't understand fully. There's nothing I can do so I just go to the next lesson and try my best.

> I usually sit there and think, 'How can I sort this question?' while the others are all writing.

If I had to pick the job I'd like to do when I leave school I'd say I would be an actor. I think I'm good at drama. When I go over the words multiple times it sticks but that takes a while, like weeks or months. Usually a couple of weeks.

I don't really mind so much finding school hard because Mum and Dad don't put pressure on me. Sometimes in lessons I feel as if I'm the odd one out and not as smart. I usually sit there and think, 'How can I sort this question?' while the others are all writing. I think, 'How can they do this so well?' When I really think about it, if I didn't have dyslexia I wouldn't struggle so much, but I don't mind having it because it's who I am.

Anwen, 10, Glamorgan, Wales

I used to be behind with my work and I used to have different work from everyone else because they were all at higher stages. I was quite young then so I didn't really mind.

When we moved up to juniors they numbered our tables one to five. Someone who works hard and understands the work was on table five and I was on table one. I wanted to be at least on table two. I was upset about that. I went home and talked to my mam and then I talked to the deputy head. She has said now we won't have numbers because some of the kids don't like them, so I think other people talked to her as well.

Schoolwork is really hard and I have two sisters and they find it really hard too. I have a teacher who helps me and sits with me sometimes at school.

The hardest thing at school is the lesson we have called 'Read Write'. It's all reading and spelling. Because we have to do it in year groups and I was behind in my year group, I find that really hard.

When my parents went to parents evening, one of teachers who does tests told them I was dyslexic and my parents told me.

I was upset at first but then I came to the dyslexia centre run by Tomorrow's Generation for extra help and I love coming here. I'm so happy, so happy I am. Here we are all together. It's not like a big class and the groups are always fun. They are really nice and come up with strategies and ways to help me remember things.

At school I'm good at History and 'topics' – learning about different subjects. I find that interesting. I also do sports: triathlon, netball, cycling, running and swimming. I want to be either at the Olympics or a scientist.

If I was a scientist I would want to do work about all the planets. I want to work on how many tiny planets there are and why they are so little. I'd like to find out why, if people can go to the moon, they can't go to the planets. I want to go to Neptune. When we learnt about the planets at school that was my favourite because it is warm and blue.

Top dyslexia tips

Leah's list: The words of wisdom of one 13-year-old

- Try your best at everything.

- Know that other people also have dyslexia and that you're not alone.

- Don't make kids sit next to the really smart people, their worst enemies, who always finish first. They should let you sit next to someone who you're good friends with. They can explain things to you in simple terms so that you can understand.

- I like studying really useful things. In ICT we have just finished Photoshop®, coding and safety on the internet. All really useful.

- Let us fiddle with stuff when we do our work. I like a piece of Blu-Tack®. It gets your mind on track.

Teachers have told me off and said, 'Give that to me.' Embarrassing.

- It's good to be active and do PE and do different stuff, not just sitting in a classroom.

- Leave a school if they don't believe you are dyslexic. We moved me from my first school. I had to wait for a space in the next school. That one was much better.

- Don't put us in a group with other people with learning difficulties when we shouldn't be in that group. I was confident in the main class. Now I'm not confident. Sometimes teachers just don't care.

- Get a good tutor. If it's a bad tutor, how's that going to help you? You're just throwing your money out of the window.

- Think about what you're good at. I'm a bit more artistic and a bit more 'out there'. I'm not that scared to try new things. I have lots of ideas all the time.

- Have animals at home. Something there to comfort you. You can talk to them. They won't listen but it makes you feel better. I used to cry every day going to school and hold on to my mum. I was upset because I couldn't read or write. When you talk to animals they have such random replies and they do random stuff like chasing their tails and going crazy after sweet wrappers and hair bands.

(Leah, 13, Surrey, England)

More top dyslexia tips

I listen to a lot of audiobooks. Sometimes I look at covers of books but don't read them and I get ideas for stories from the covers. Even studying advertisements for books gives me inspiration. *(Rocco, 11, Hertfordshire, England)*

Read books that have been out for a while. This means the colour of the pages is a bit duller and much easier to read than newly printed white pages. The pages aren't yellow but they aren't white either. *(Molly, 16, Stirlingshire, Scotland)*

If I read a book and don't understand a word on the page, I write on a sticky note and put it underneath the word so I can check it later. *(Katelynn, 15, Michigan, USA)*

I used to look at the pictures in the book and think what the words would be. When I went to bed my mammy would read me a book, I would look at the pictures and get the words. That's what I did to learn to read. *(James, 9, County Kildare, Ireland)*

You have to work hard at things like punctuation and spelling, but it's so important to concentrate on your strengths. Focusing only on your negatives just won't help you. *(Sam, 16, London, England)*

One thing that helps me is reading quotations that are encouraging and inspiring, especially when I am feeling upset or despondent. *(JX, 14, Hougang, Singapore)*

I use a Kindle and blow the text up to as big a size as possible. I'm a slow reader so when I do this it feels like I'm getting through the books really quickly because there are so few words on a page! I avoid words I can't remember and just say 'thingy'. *(Daisy, 14, West Sussex, England)*

My mom made me study plans and, because she knew I lose concentration fast, she factored in lots of breaks. *(Jarred, 14, Aruba, The Caribbean)*

Never take no for an answer if you need something. We are short of coloured paper in my region. It makes a great difference for some people if they can write on and read from coloured paper. *(Elliot, 17, Stirlingshire, Scotland)*

Time management is essential for me. I love a good list with achievable goals. *(Isobel, 17, Vale of Glamorgan, Wales)*

My mother celebrated even the slightest incremental improvement in my marks, even if I was failing miserably. She always told me that as long as I have tried my very best she will be very pleased. This message makes me want to work even harder. *(JX, 14, Hougang, Singapore)*

What teachers shouldn't do
(according to the true experts)

Don't teach kids with dyslexia as if they are other kids. They will not learn as quickly as the teacher is teaching. Then they start to question why they don't understand, why they don't learn what the others are learning and then they don't go to school and they stay at home feeling like there's no one else like them. *(Phoebe, 10, Victoria, Australia)*

One teacher skips through everything really quickly and then gives us a test out of the blue. Not inspirational. *(Leah, 14, London, England)*

The worst thing a teacher can do is not understand that you are trying your best. They may think we're not, but we are. *(Abby, 10, Illinois, USA)*

They do this thing called popcorn reading. One person starts reading and once they have read something they say 'popcorn' and say someone else's name and that person has to carry on. I don't like it if it's my turn because I get something wrong or I skip a line or two. *(Rachel, 11, London, England)*

Teachers should definitely not rush kids with dyslexia and they should let us have extra time for our work. When I was in first grade I felt like I was rushed all the time. If I'm rushed my mind goes all wild and doesn't know what to do and what I'm supposed to do next. *(Jed, 10, Texas, USA)*

Some teachers would make me stand up in front of the class and read out my answers or my scores. *(Max, 17, Bay of Plenty, New Zealand)*

I find it embarrassing when the teacher asks me questions in front of the class and I can't answer. Sometimes she asks me to read in front of the class and I find this embarrassing too. *(Fiona, 9, County Kildare, Ireland)*

The worst thing a teacher can do is to put down children with dyslexia with negative words. *(Ramu, 9, Madras, India)*

One teacher 'leaves us to read' in class. I try but the information doesn't go into my brain at all. Instead I use a highlighter and take it home to read later. *(Charlie, 17, London, England)*

The worst thing a teacher can do is shout, 'I don't want any spelling mistakes. I want you to get these words all right.' *(Callum, 9, Renfrewshire, Scotland)*

Sometimes they put the pile of marked papers right in front so everyone going to get theirs can see your mark which is written with a circle round it. *(Leah, 14, London, England)*

One problem is when teachers don't write on the board, but read something out to the class. When it's bigger words or a sentence it's hard for me to write. *(Kane, 15, Merthyr Tydfil, Wales)*

The worst thing is when the teachers give you more work for homework and don't explain how to do it. You are meant to figure it out for yourself. *(Miles, 13, Victoria, Australia)*

The worst thing a teacher can do is yell. You can't talk back because they think talking back is rude and then you get detention. *(Addison, 11, Ohio, USA)*

The worst thing a teacher can do is judge you on the grades you scored when you were young. Once things start to change they should never look at your previous grades. *(Hannah, 18, London, England)*

School was kind of helpful when giving me the extra time but not so helpful in giving me methods to try to make up for what I'm lacking. *(Charlie, 17, London, England)*

The worst thing a teacher can do is help you too much. You know how to do it and then your teacher tells you how to do it. I think they underestimate me. *(Lucy, 11, Bay of Plenty, New Zealand)*

The worst thing the teachers used to say to me when I asked for help was, 'No I can't do this for you.' I wasn't asking them to do it for me. I just need to learn. I was asking for help. *(Samuel, 12, New Brunswick, Canada)*

The worst thing is to tell the entire class that a student has dyslexia or other special learning needs without finding out beforehand if the affected student actually minds about them revealing it. Sometimes, giving such students too much attention is also not a very good idea as the others may feel that the teachers are showing favouritism in class. *(JX, 14, Hougang, Singapore)*

What teachers should do (according to the true experts)

Sometimes the teacher spends more time with me and I get printouts to help me and prompt me. *(Rocco, 11, Hertfordshire, England)*

The best things the teachers can do is to help me try to learn and give me all the tools I need. Getting the help has put up my grades. It's helped me to learn the way I know how to learn. *(Samuel, 12, New Brunswick, Canada)*

Teachers have to be patient, very patient. *(Sam, 16, London, England)*

If I was running a school I would provide a space so that people with some form of dyslexia could go there and be tested and they could find better ways to help you. *(Charlie, 17, London, England)*

Teachers should ask the kids with dyslexia how they want to be taught. Sit down and ask them what works for them. There is no same strategy that works for two people. *(Elliot, 17, Stirlingshire, Scotland)*

The best thing teachers can do is sit them down and explain to them what the consonant is and what the vowel is. Break up words so they can understand. *(Phoebe, 10, Victoria, Australia)*

The best thing teachers can do is leave you to be. I like being left alone when I'm doing my work. The person next to me can help because she's my friend. *(Lucy, 11, Bay of Plenty, New Zealand)*

I think teachers should ask children how they like to be taught. Do they like hands-on teaching or is it useful to use games that help you to remember? *(Eddie, 14, Manchester, England)*

The teachers give me work in smaller sections and that helps. *(Leah, 14, London, England)*

If there's a lot of writing sometimes I ask the teacher if they will come and write it down for me. In one subject the teacher sometimes prints off the PowerPoint for me. *(Jamie, 12, Glasgow, Scotland)*

School recently gave me some stuff to help me with reading – a reading ruler and some overlays and also a yellow board, which is easier to read from. *(Ella, 11, Manchester, England)*

In the lessons I have been put in slightly smaller groups because when I was working with larger groups of 30 I didn't understand. *(Sonny, 13, Buckinghamshire, England)*

Teachers should cut some slack about writing homework, and how and when it is done. They should never give up on us. *(Freddie, 10, London, England)*

My SpLD [Specific Learning Difficulties] teacher has given me a laminated pass to show supply teachers who don't know me. They know then to write things down for me or give me a hand-out. Most of my teachers know to give me hand-outs. Teachers who don't know me is one of the main problems. *(Kane, 15, Merthyr Tydfil, Wales)*

If I am taking an exam in a small room I feel I can relax more than in a big room with lots of people turning over the page and writing far more than me. *(Daisy, 14, West Sussex, England)*

Right now I have a lovely teacher who makes math interesting and funny. He gets us to take PE every day so we get lots of little breaks and this helps me concentrate. *(Amelia, 12, Victoria, Canada)*

The most important thing that teachers can do is give us more time. We also need more time in tests. *(Abby, 10, Illinois, USA)*

In New Zealand we have this test called the star test, which is maths, English and reading all in one. Just as an experiment the teacher let me sit it without the usual time constraints. I did really well. It didn't count as my score, but it did make me feel more confident. *(Lucy, 11, Bay of Plenty, New Zealand)*

Teachers should celebrate with their students, even if their improvements seem to be insignificant. If the students are still failing, the teachers should be kind, caring and loving to them by giving them further assistance so that they can clarify their doubts in order to perform better the next time round. *(JX, 14, Hougang, Singapore)*

Special thanks to

Ann Rappaport

Aggie MacKenzie

Charles Freeman

David Sheridan

Delia Gascoigne and The Dyslexia Clinic, London

DRC Generations, Glasgow, Scotland

Dyslexia Association of Ireland, including Rosie Bissett

Dyslexia Association of Singapore, including Deborah
     Hewes

Dyslexia Foundation of New Zealand, including Esther
     Whitehead

Dyslexia Scotland, including Katie Carmichael, Louise
     Comrie, Roisin McCusker, James Brown and Pamela
     Holmes

Geraldine Durcan

Jenny Crook

Karen Pilling

Karen Starkiss, Dyslexia Assessment and Support
    Services, Australia

Laura Hendry, Bedford Modern School

Lauren Milberger

Liz Robin

Loretta Magennis, for your support and ideas

Madras Dyslexia Association, including Harini Ramanujam

Members of Dyslexia Help and Support UK
    Facebook group

Members of Dyslexia Support Australia Facebook group

Members of Dyslexia Support – for Parents of Dyslexic
    Children Facebook group

Michael Crook

Natasha Henson

Nathalie Parry

Nicole Sochor

Norma Blecker

Ryan Hamilton Black, for the title and chat

Saffron Cooksey, Dyslexia/SpLD teacher, Cardiff

St Mary's RC Primary School, Manchester, including
    Mylene McGuire and Joanne Mulryan

Sarah Asome, Bentleigh West Primary School, Victoria,
    Australia

'The Amazing Dyslexics' Kate Power and Kathy Forsyth

The Codpast, the dyslexia podcast: Sean Douglas and
    Bitzy Au

The Stokey mums!

Tomorrow's Generation Dyslexia Centre, Cardiff, including
    Helen Grimes, Debbie Lazell, Carole Bradley and
    Banaeshia Tooley
Walthamstow Dyslexia Association
Wendy Searle
WJ Turner School, Fort Worth ISD, Texas, especially
    Ashley Tejeda
Zoe Taylor

Creative, Successful, Dyslexic

23 High Achievers Share Their Stories

Margaret Rooke

Foreword by Mollie King

ISBN 978 1 84905 653 3 (hardback)
ISBN 978 1 78592 060 8 (paperback)
eISBN 978 1 78450 163 1

What do the following people have in common: Darcey Bussell CBE, Eddie Izzard, David Bailey CBE, Sir Richard Branson, Zoe Wanamaker CBE, Richard Rogers and Benjamin Zephaniah?

They're all well-known, successful and dyslexic.

Featuring first-person stories from 23 well-known people, this inspiring book shows that dyslexia doesn't have to be a barrier to success. Indeed, it can bring with it the determination, creativity and outlook needed to achieve all we want in life.

'This book provides clear and inspirational hope for anyone with a dyslexic child. Like many excellent books it is written from personal experience. I strongly recommend it.'

– *Sian Griffiths, Education Editor,* The Sunday Times

'This collection of very personal stories from such high profile dyslexic people brought together in one book will act as an inspiration for those who struggle daily with dyslexia and also as an eye opener to those that don't. It will help them to better understand the impact that a learning difficulty can have on everyday life and the importance of providing appropriate emotional and practical support.'

– *Stephen Hall, Chief Executive, Dyslexia Action*

'I would recommend this to people diagnosed with dyslexia and their families. One invaluable message is that perseverance and determination can help people achieve. Another is that talents in the dyslexia profile may be underrated at school but are of tremendous importance to society afterwards.'

– *Bernadette McLean, Principal of the Helen Arkell Dyslexia Centre, UK*

'A wonderful book.'

– *Dr Brock Eide and Dr Fernette Eide, authors of* The Dyslexic Advantage: Unlocking the Hidden Potential of the Dyslexic Brain